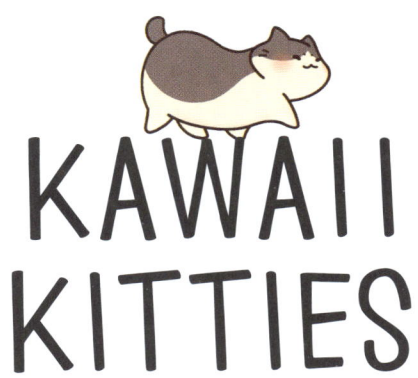

KAWAII KITTIES

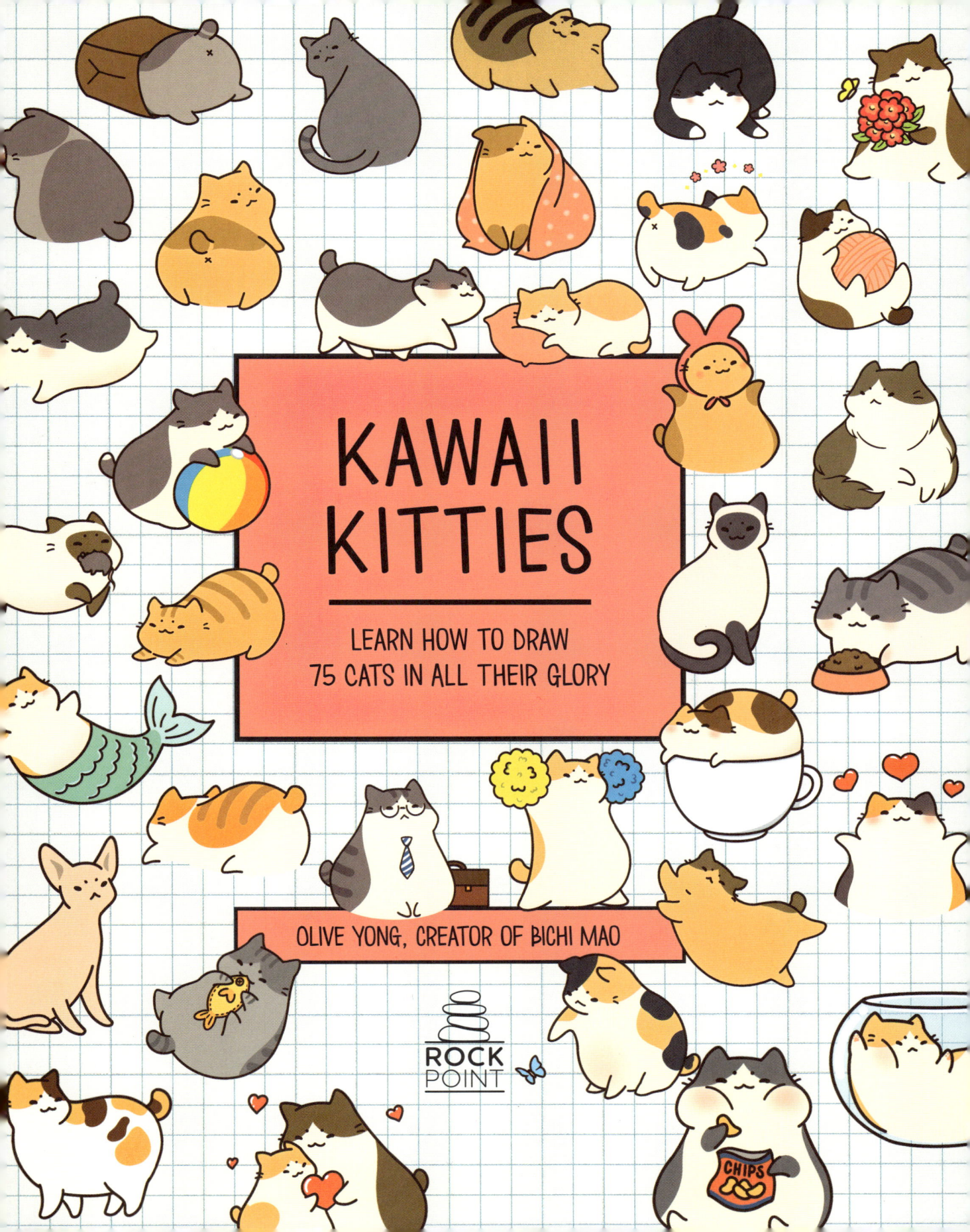

KAWAII KITTIES

LEARN HOW TO DRAW
75 CATS IN ALL THEIR GLORY

OLIVE YONG, CREATOR OF BICHI MAO

ROCK
POINT

First published in 2021 by Rock Point, an imprint of The Quarto Group,
142 West 36th Street, 4th Floor, New York, NY 10018, USA
T (212) 779-4972 www.Quarto.com

Rock Point titles are also available at discount for retail, wholesale, promotional and bulk purchase.
For details, contact the Special Sales Manager by email at specialsales@quarto.com or by mail at
The Quarto Group, Attn: Special Sales Manager, 100 Cummings Center Suite, 265D, Beverly, MA 01915, USA.

20

ISBN: 978-1-63106-739-6

Library of Congress Control Number: 2020945070

Publisher: Rage Kindelsperger
Creative Director: Laura Drew
Managing Editor: Cara Donaldson
Senior Editor: Erin Canning
Cover and Interior Design: Kim Winscher

Printed in China

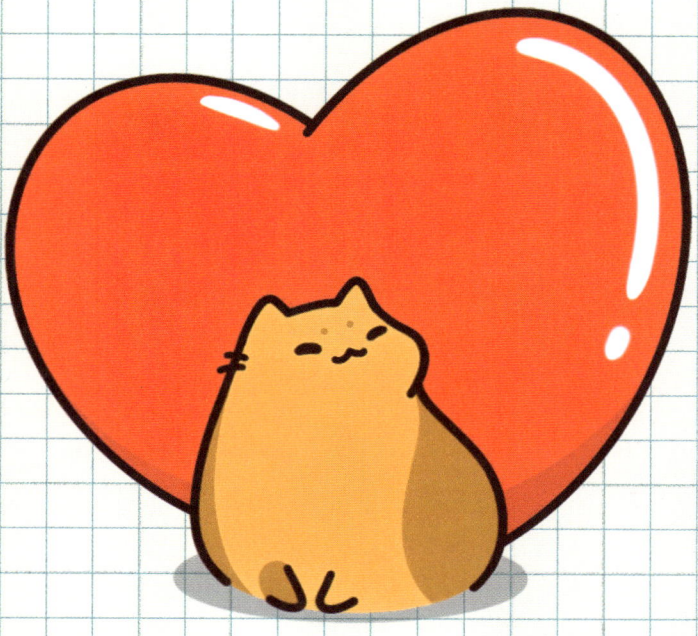

This book is dedicated to my family, who always supported my passion for creating art and believing in me. To my partner, Wee Lim, who not only inspired and introduced me to the digital medium, but who has also been patient and encouraging throughout my journey. To all my Bichi Mao comic readers, who enjoy my work and share it with the world. To my editor, Erin, and the team at The Quarto Group, who gave me this great opportunity and showed me the ropes through publishing my first book. Lastly, I want to say thank you to myself for not giving up and persevering through today. W. Clement Stone once said, "Aim for the moon. If you miss, you may hit a star."

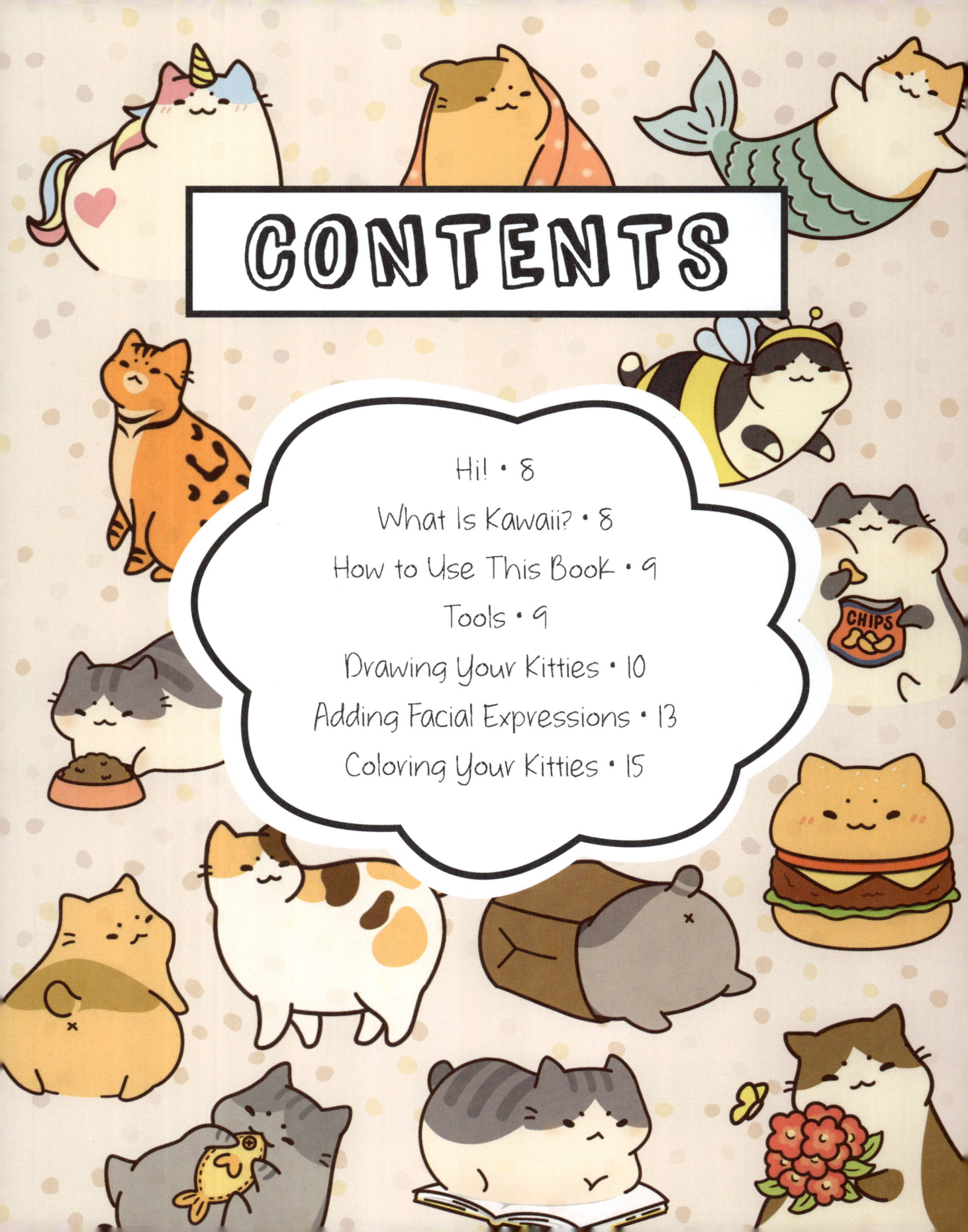

CONTENTS

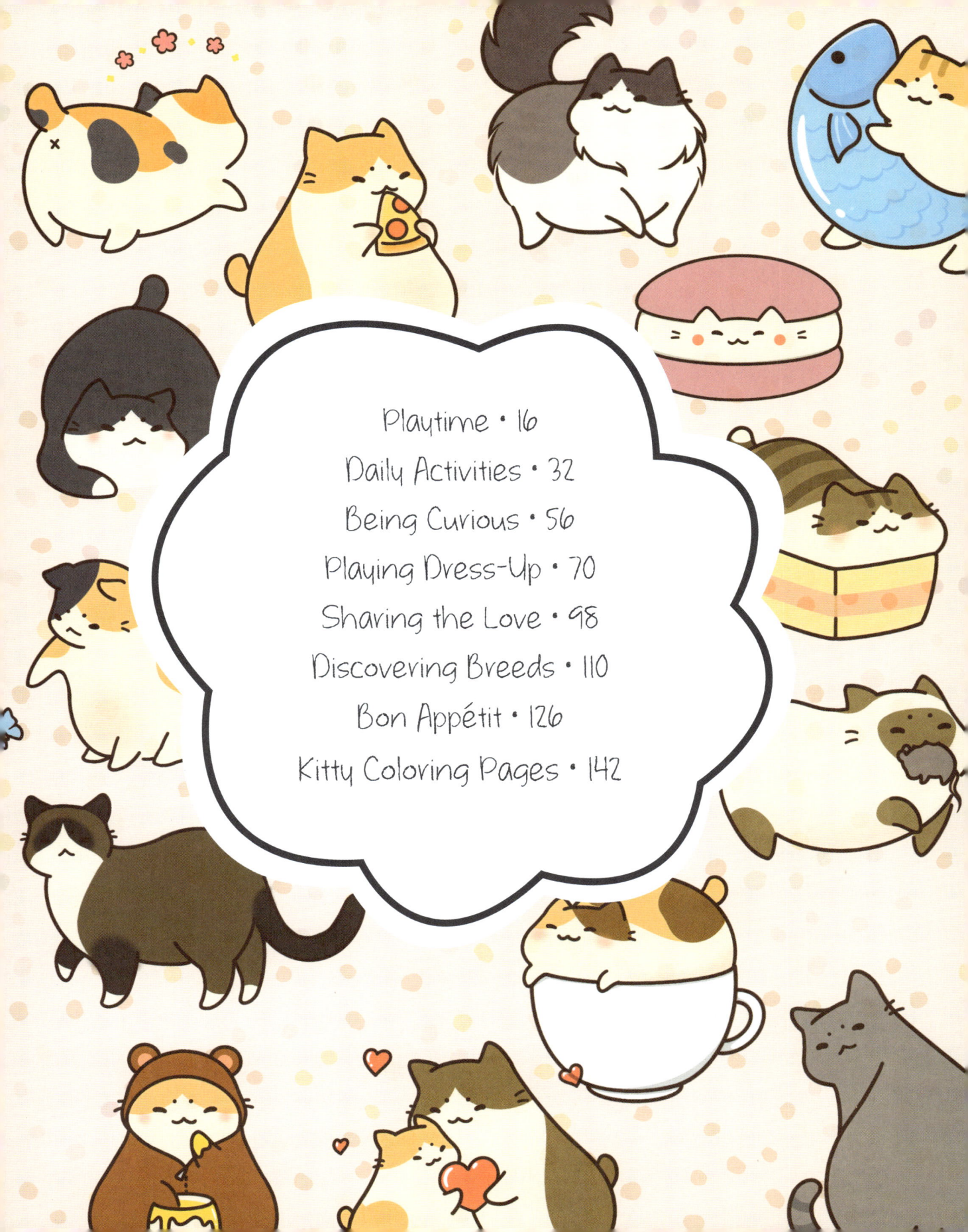

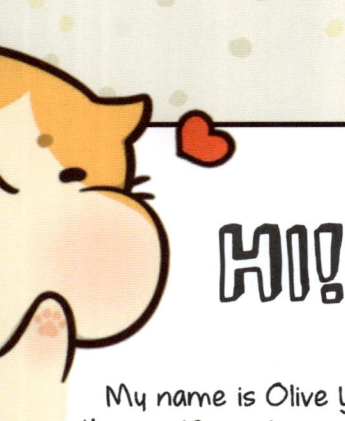

HI!

My name is Olive Yong, and I'm a self-taught artist from Malaysia. Drawing has always been a passion of mine, and I mostly work with pencil and paper. In June 2019, I was introduced to digital drawing and started working with the Procreate program on the iPad. From there, I began to post my art across social media platforms under the name Bichi Mao. Within a year, Bichi Mao has amassed a large following. I'm really surprised that people enjoy and love what I'm doing, and their support gives me strength to continue creating.

Bichi Mao is a cute and relatable webcomic series revolving around cat characters presented in an adorable and simplistic art style, like the kitties you'll learn how to draw in this book! Through my comics, I try to portray everyday ups and downs. What motivates me to keep drawing and sharing my art is that I want to continue spreading positivity and make people smile. I also enjoy sharing my views on certain topics to bring awareness to the public in hopes of helping to make the world a little kinder.

I hope that this book inspires you to not only learn how to draw these adorable kitties, but also to create your own characters, whether they are cats or something entirely different.

What Is Kawaii?

You might have heard the word. You have probably seen the hashtag. You definitely know the style. But what, exactly, does Kawaii mean?

Kawaii is a Japanese concept or idea, dating back to the 1970s, that translates closely to "cuteness" in English. In Japan, the usage of the word is quite broad and can be used to describe anything cute, from clothing and accessories to handwriting and art. So, if you are a fan of emoji art or the style of beloved characters like Hello Kitty, Pokémon, or Pusheen the Cat, then you already know and love the Kawaii style of art!

While there are many interpretations as to what constitutes the "Kawaii" art aesthetic, most people can agree that Kawaii art is usually composed of very simple black outlines, pastel colors, and characters or objects with a rounded, youthful appearance. Facial expressions in Kawaii art are minimal and characters are frequently drawn with oversized heads and smaller bodies.

How to Use This Book

After some helpful information here in the beginning of the book about tools and drawing techniques, there are seventy-five step-by-step tutorials divided into seven sections: Playtime, Daily Activities, Being Curious, Playing Dress-Up, Sharing the Love, Discovering Breeds, and Bon Appétit. At the end of the book are Kitty Coloring Pages with lots of kawaii kitties for you to color and decorate.

Tools

Feel free to draw your kawaii kitties with whatever you have available to you, but here are some suggestions.

TRADITIONAL TOOLS
If you're drawing your cats with traditional tools, use a pencil, such as a 2B/HB (#2 pencil) for the initial sketch, and then use a black ink pen to finish your drawing—once your sketch is final. You may want to invest in a high-quality eraser to easily get rid of any unwanted lines and marks. A ruler may also be helpful for when you're working with straight lines.

For coloring your kitties, I recommend using color pencils, crayons, or watercolors. Have fun experimenting with what works best for you. The coloring pages on pages 142 and 143 are a great place to practice!

DIGITAL TOOLS
There are a number of software programs and apps for drawing digitally, whether you prefer drawing on a desktop, laptop, or iPad. Like I mentioned earlier, I prefer using Procreate on an iPad, but see what works best for your artwork, equipment, and budget.

Regarding the brushes included with these programs, I like the Monoline brush in Procreate, but again, have fun experimenting.

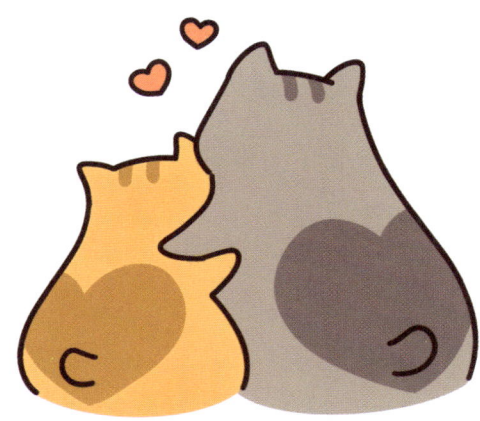

DRAWING YOUR KITTIES

I like to use a lot of curved lines in my drawings, which help contribute to that kawaii, or cuteness, factor. Here are the basic shapes you will see throughout the tutorials in this book.

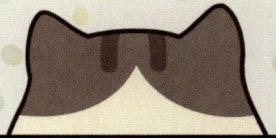

Body Types

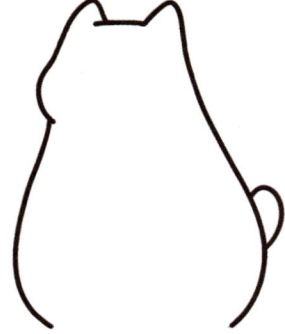
Slim

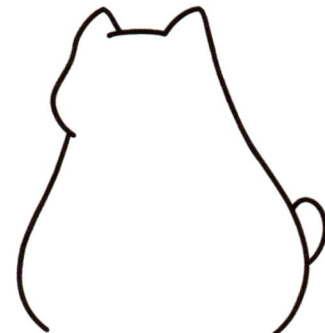
Average

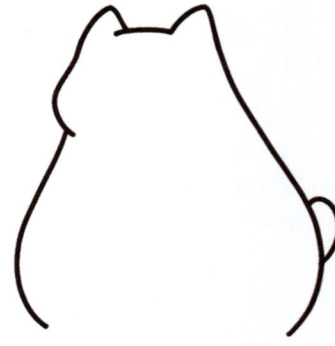
Chonk

. . . .

Head Shape

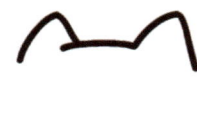 + 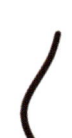 =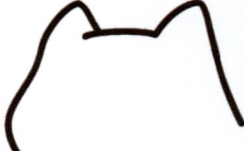

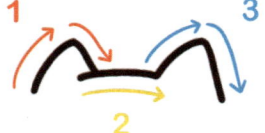 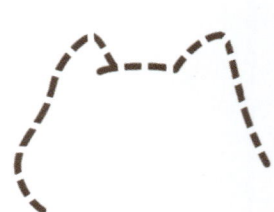

Try it out!

Body Shapes

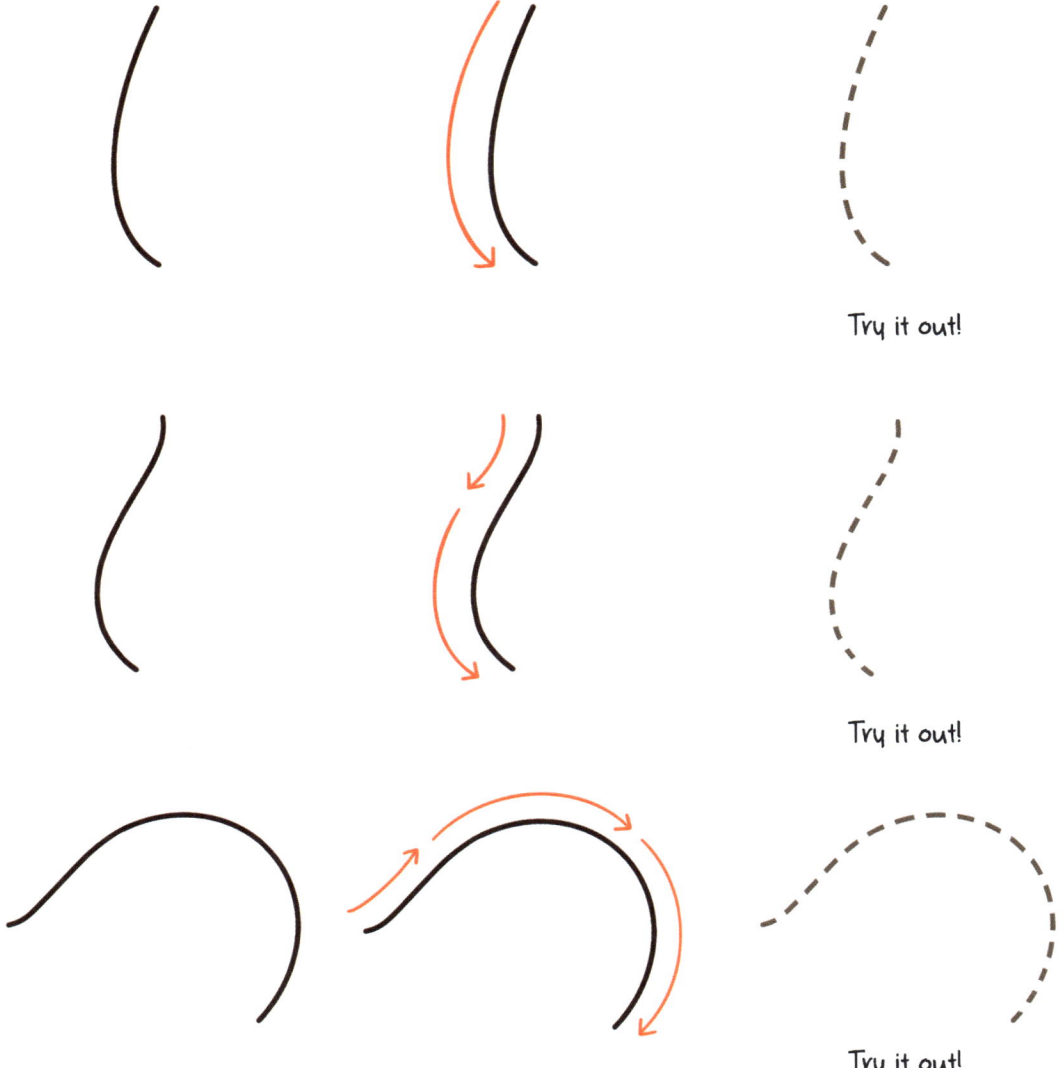

Try it out!

Try it out!

Try it out!

Leg Shapes

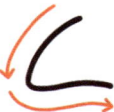

Try it out!

Try it out!

Try it out!

Tail Shapes

 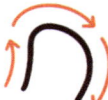

Try it out!

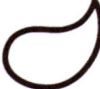 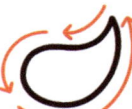 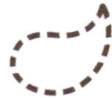

Try it out!

ADDING FACIAL EXPRESSIONS

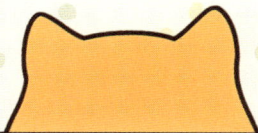

Facial expressions are what give these kitties their Kawaii factor. Here, I show you how to place the facial features on your kitties' heads and include a directory of some of my favorite facial expressions on the following page.

Facial Expression Placement

1.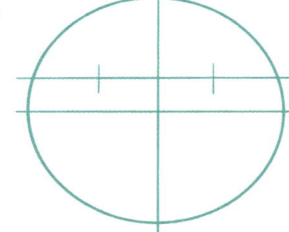

2.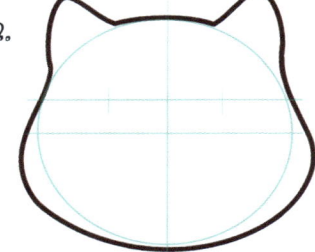

3.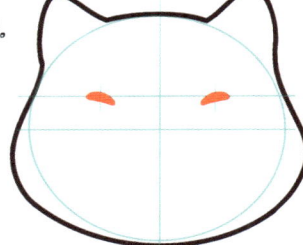

4.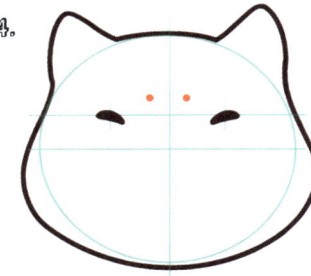

5.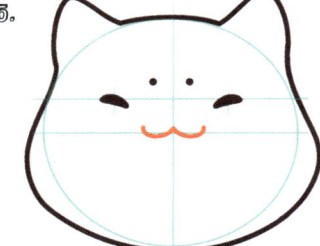

6.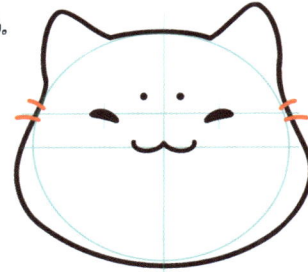

7.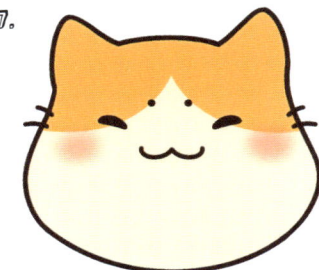

Try it out!

13

FACIAL EXPRESSION DIRECTORY

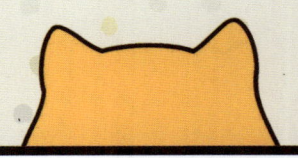

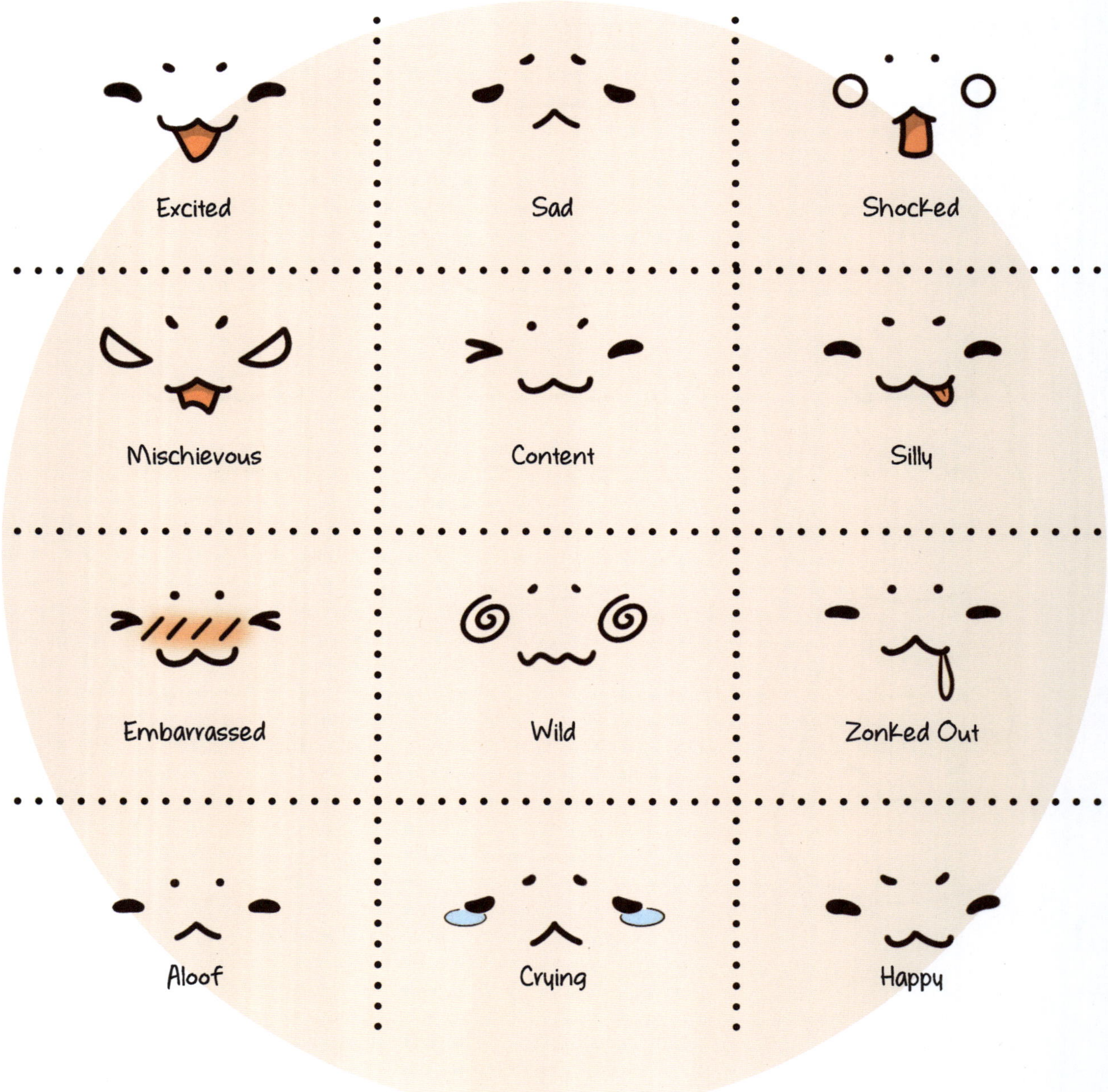

Excited

Sad

Shocked

Mischievous

Content

Silly

Embarrassed

Wild

Zonked Out

Aloof

Crying

Happy

COLORING YOUR KITTIES

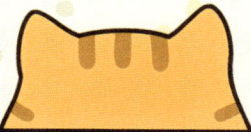

These are the colors and markings I prefer to use on my kitties, but you can make your kitties any color and pattern you want, even beyond what is realistic. Don't forget to practice using the coloring pages on pages 142 and 143!

Color Palette

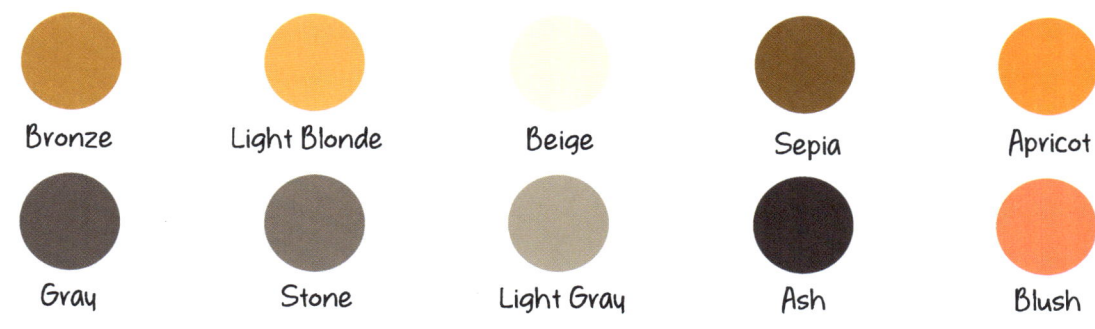

Bronze	Light Blonde	Beige	Sepia	Apricot
Gray	Stone	Light Gray	Ash	Blush

Head Markings

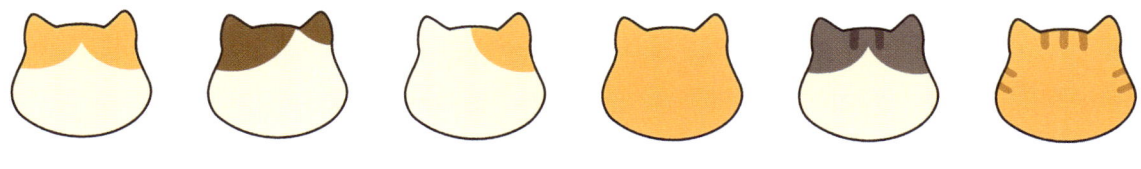

Body Markings

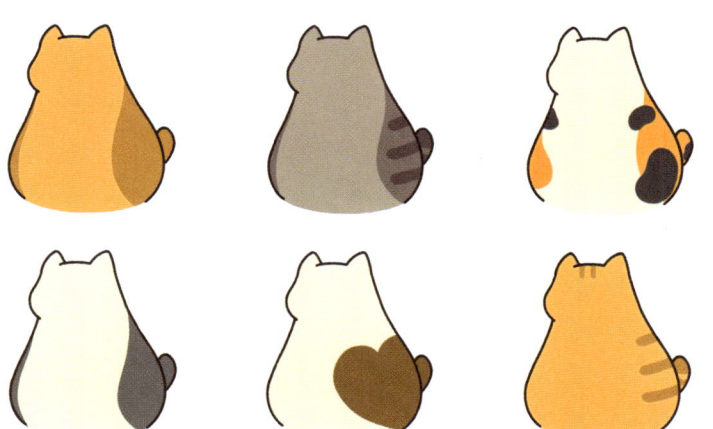

PLAYTIME

Happiness is like a butterfly.
The more you chase it,
the more it will elude you.

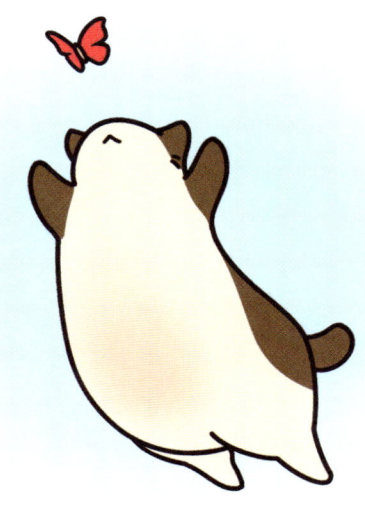

But if you turn your attention to other things,
it will come and sit softly on your shoulder.

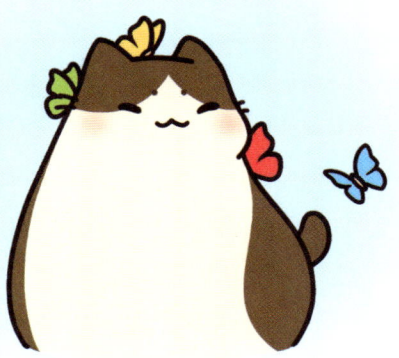

THE BALLER

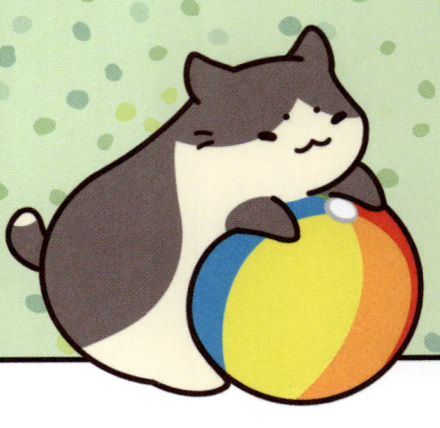

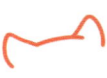

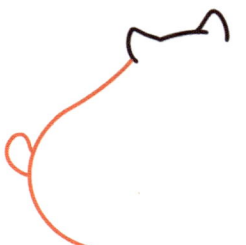

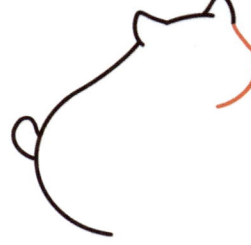

1. Draw the top of the head and the ears slightly tilted to the left.

2. Draw the back of the body. Add the tail.

3. Draw the right side of the head.

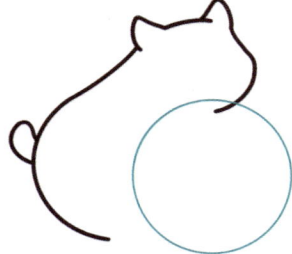

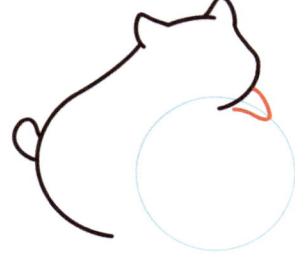

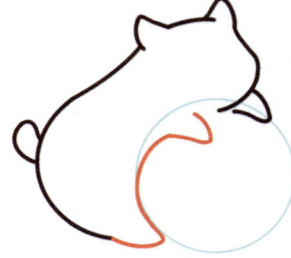

4. Draw a circle for the outline of the beach ball that overlaps the front of the body.

5. Place a front leg on top of the beach ball.

6. Draw a curved line around the beach ball for the kitty's body, extending it into the front and back legs.

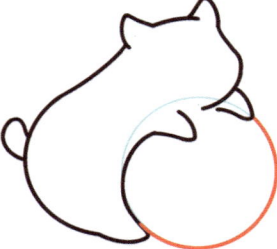

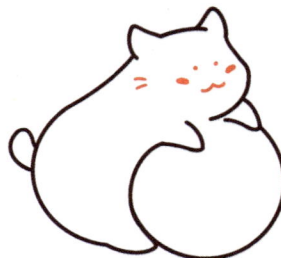

7. Draw a semicircle for the shape of the beach ball.

8. Finish by giving your kitty a fun facial expression.

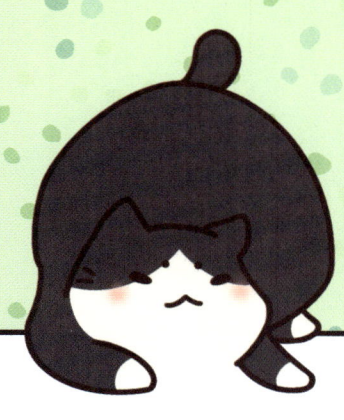

THE POUNCER

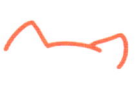

1. Draw the top of the head and the ears slightly tilted to the right.

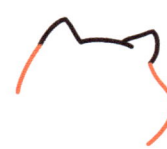

2. Draw the sides of the head.

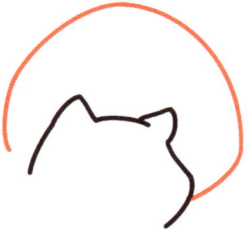

3. Draw an arc around the head for the body.

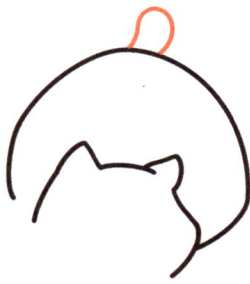

4. Add the tail.

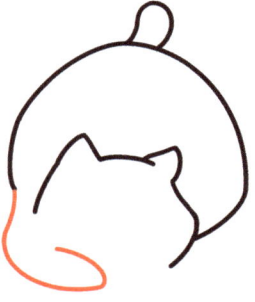

5. Draw the front leg, extending from the left side of the body.

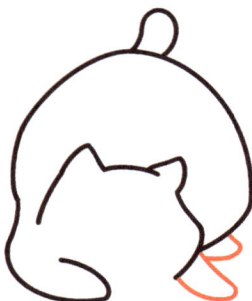

6. Draw the front and back legs on the right side.

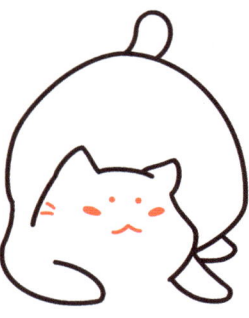

7. Finish by giving your kitty a fun facial expression.

THE MOUSER

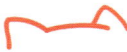

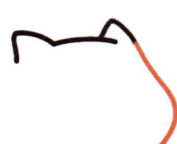

1. Draw the top of the head and the ears slightly tilted backward.

2. Draw the right side of the head.

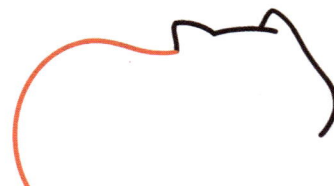

3. Draw the back of the body.

4. Draw the leg, extending it from the back of the body. Add the tail.

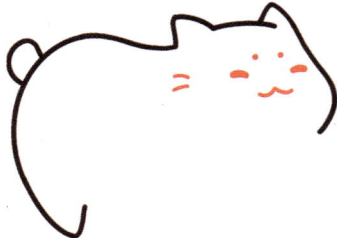

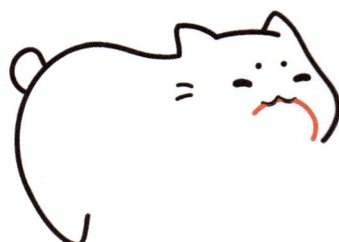

5. Give your kitty a fun facial expression.

6. Start drawing the mouse in the kitty's mouth, with a curved line for its back.

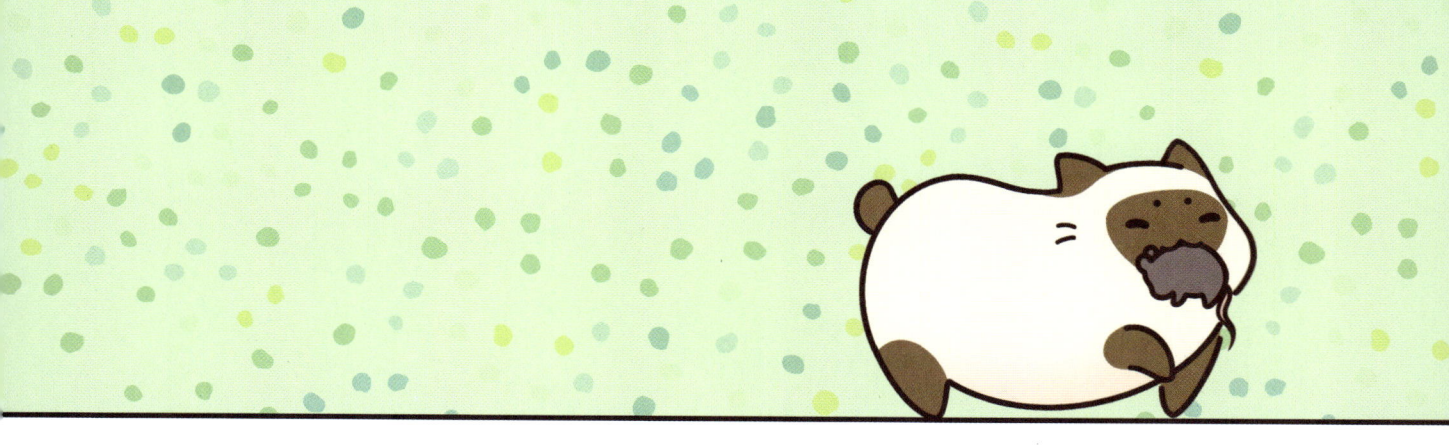

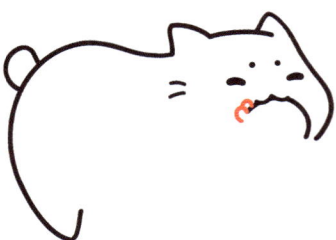

7. Add the ears.

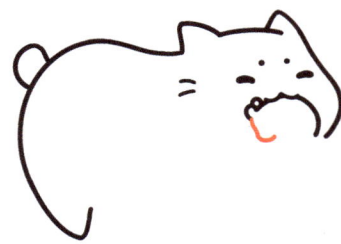

8. Draw the mouse's head.

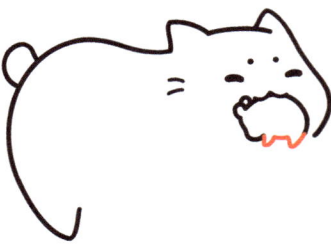

9. Draw the underside of the body and the feet.

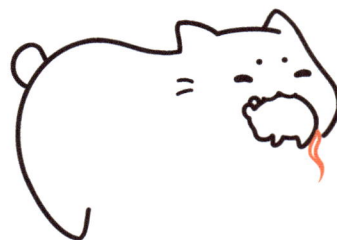

10. Add the mouse's tail.

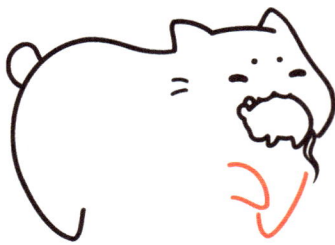

11. Draw your kitty's front legs to show a walking motion, with the leg on the left side raised and the right one extended.

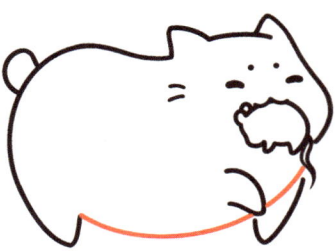

12. Finish by drawing your kitty's underside.

THE CHASER

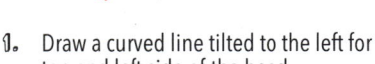

1. Draw a curved line tilted to the left for the top and left side of the head.

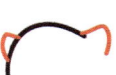

2. Add the ears.

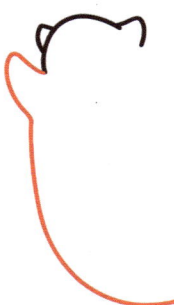

3. Draw the front of the body with the front leg raised.

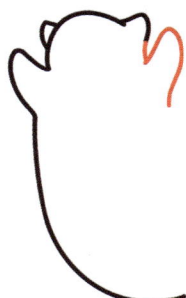

4. Draw the right side of the head, with the other front leg raised.

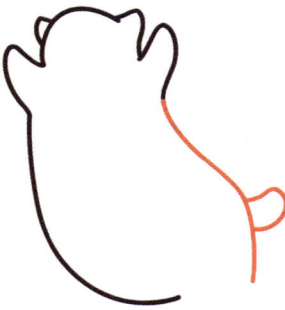

5. Draw the back of the body. Add the tail.

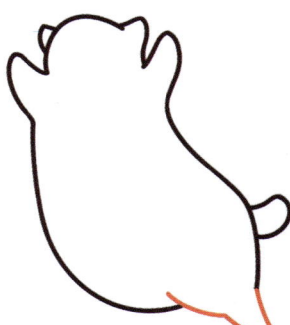

6. Add an extended back leg on the right side.

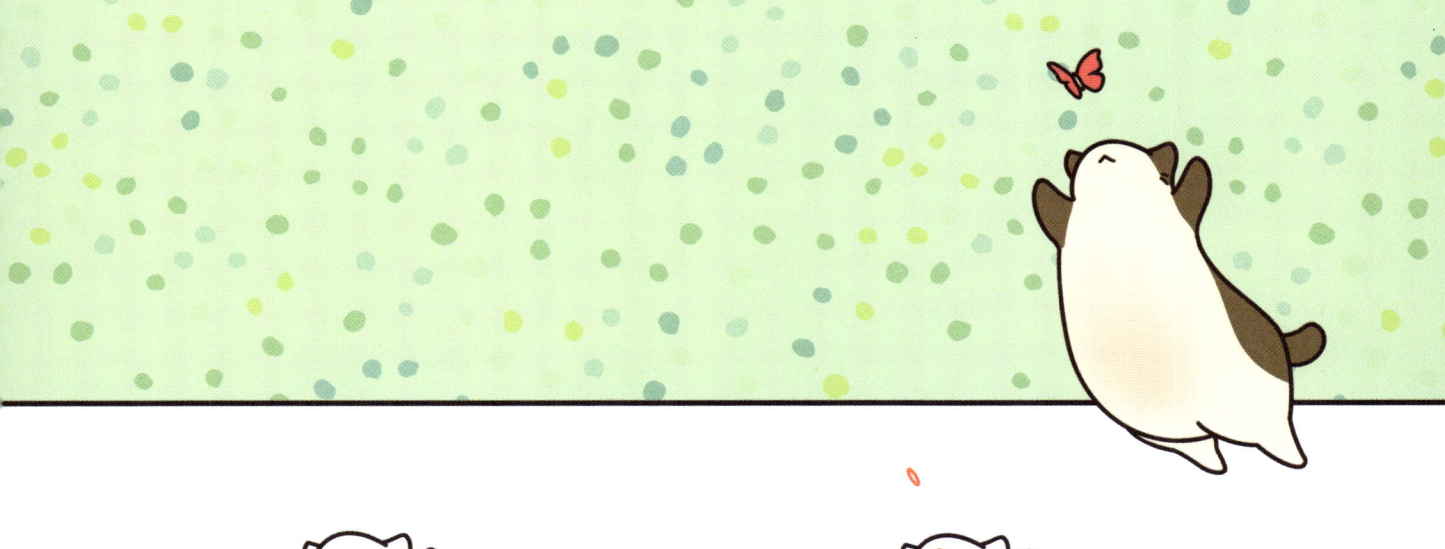

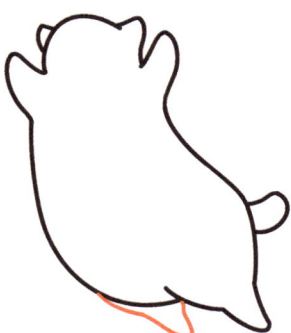

7. Draw an extended back leg on the left side.

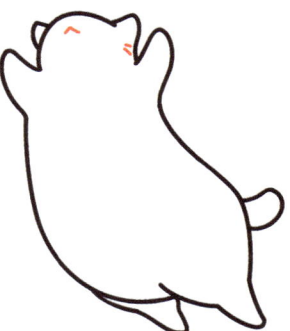

8. Place the nose on the upper part of the face and some whiskers on the right side. Draw a tiny oval above your kitty for the butterfly's body.

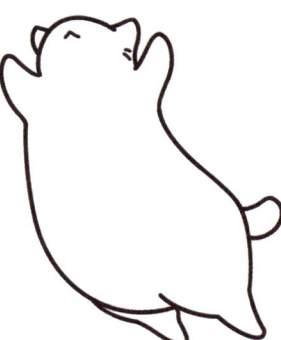

9. Add the forewings to the butterfly.

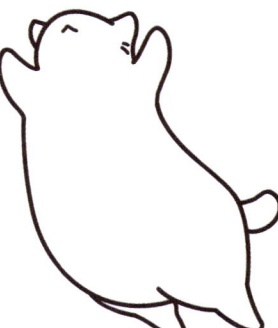

10. Finish by drawing the butterfly's hindwings.

THE KICKER

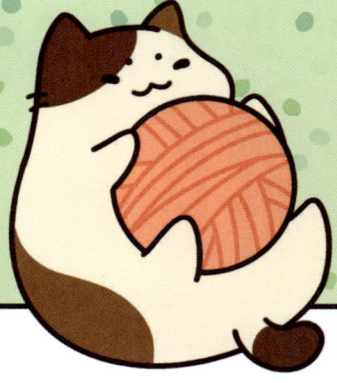

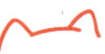

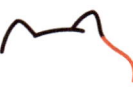

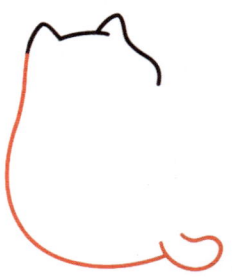

1. Draw the top of the head and the ears slightly tilted to the left.

2. Draw the right side of the head.

3. Draw the back of the body with the tail.

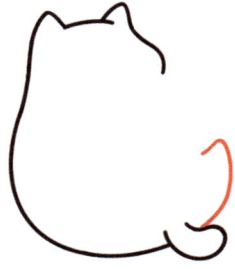

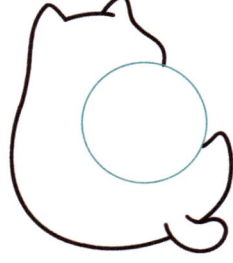

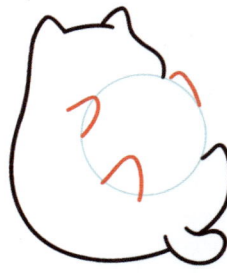

4. Draw the front of the body with the back leg raised.

5. Draw a circle for the outline of the ball of yarn that overlaps the front of the body.

6. Add the other three legs "wrapped" around the yarn ball.

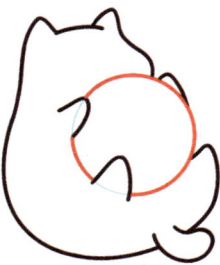

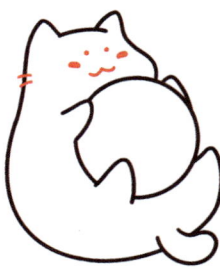

7. Draw the shape of the ball of yarn.

8. Finish by giving your kitty a fun facial expression.

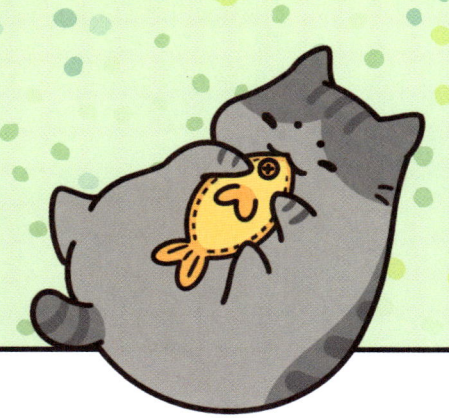

THE CHEWER

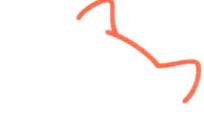

1. Draw the top of the head and the ears tilted to the right.

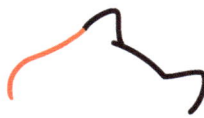

2. Draw the left side of the head.

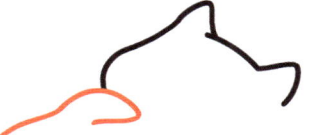

3. Draw the front of the body with the leg positioned below the head.

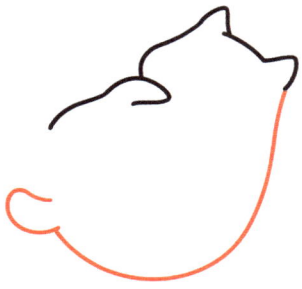

4. Draw the back of the body with the tail.

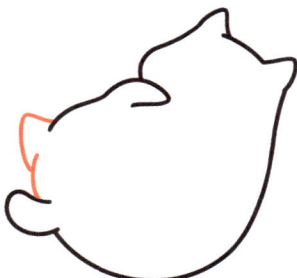

5. Complete the body, extending the line into the back leg that is kicking out.

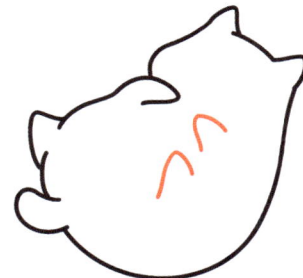

6. Draw the outer-front and -back legs on the right side.

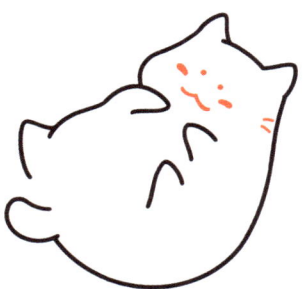

7. Give your kitty a fun facial expression.

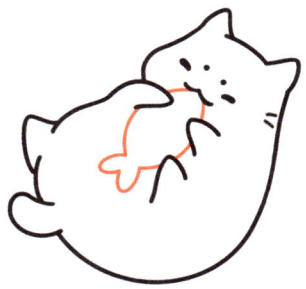

8. Draw a fish shape in the center of the kitty's body that is being "held" by the legs.

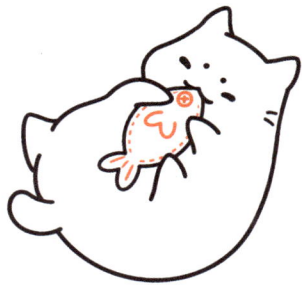

9. Finish by adding some fun details to the fish toy.

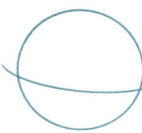

1. Draw a circle for the outline of the head, with a horizontal line across the center to help with placing the face.

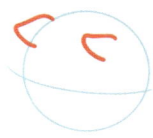

2. Draw the ears farther down on the head and tilted forward, because the kitty is looking down.

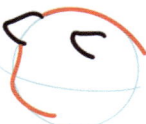

3. Draw the front and back of the head.

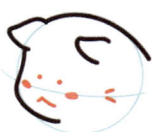

4. Give your kitty a fun facial expression, placing the eyes and whiskers on the horizontal guideline.

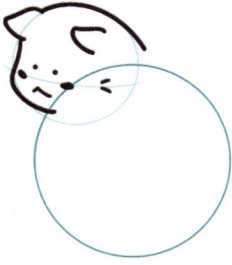

5. Draw a larger circle, overlapping the head, for the outline of the body.

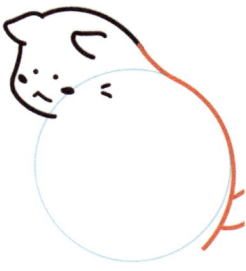

6. Draw the back of the body. Add the tail.

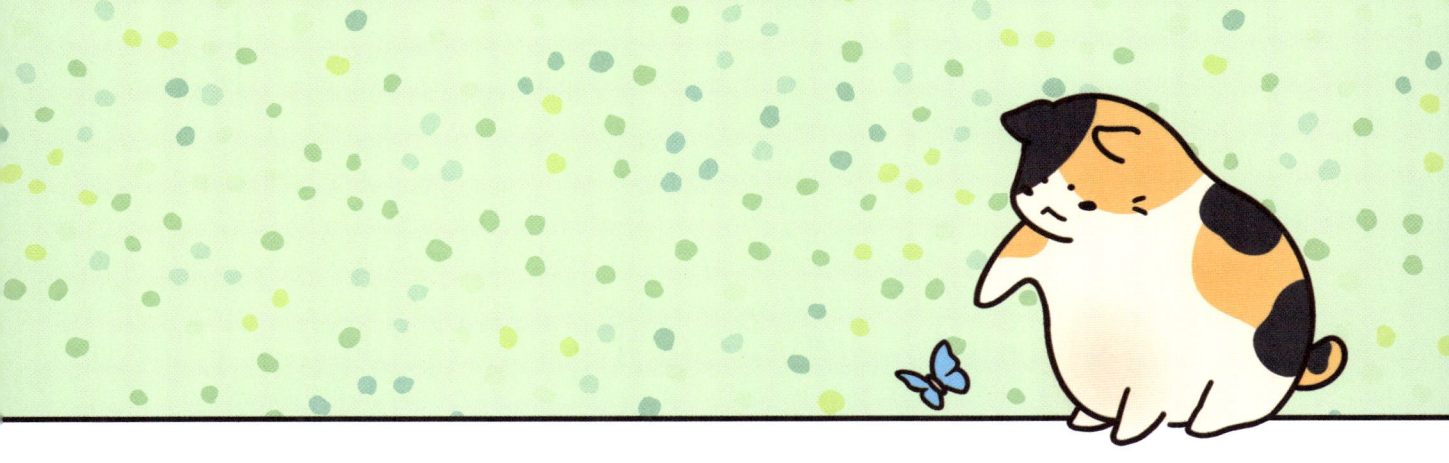

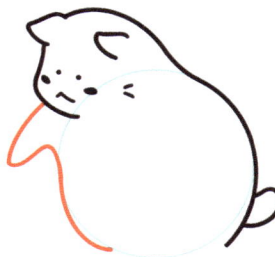

7. Draw the front of the body with the front leg raised.

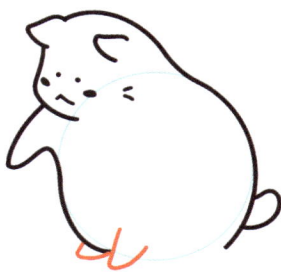

8. Add the outer-front and inner-back legs.

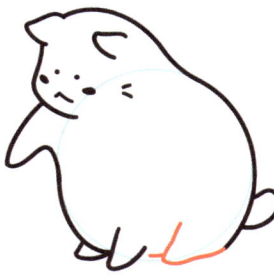

9. Draw the underside of the body and the outer-back leg.

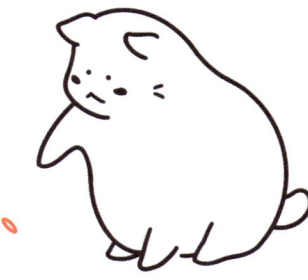

10. Draw a tiny oval diagonally below the raised front leg for the butterfly's body.

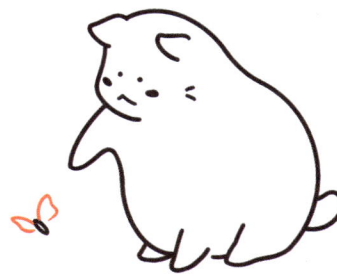

11. Add the forewings of the butterfly.

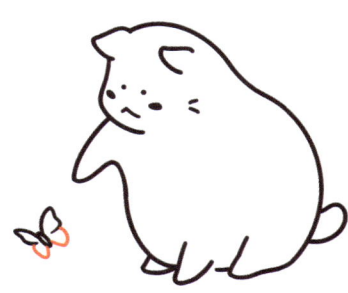

12. Finish by drawing the butterfly's hindwings.

THE COMMUNICATOR

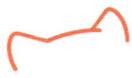

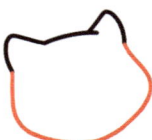

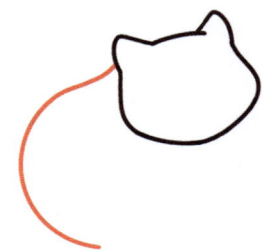

1. Draw the top of the head and the ears slightly tilted to the left.

2. Draw the rest of the head.

3. Draw the back of the body.

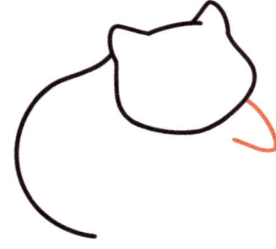

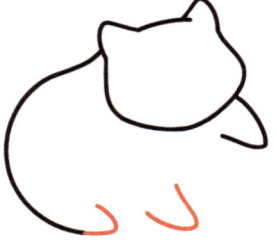

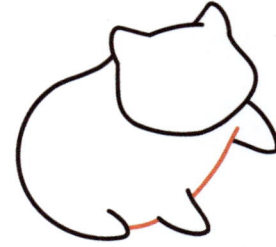

4. Draw the inner-front leg raised.

5. Draw the outer-front and -back legs.

6. Draw the underside of the body.

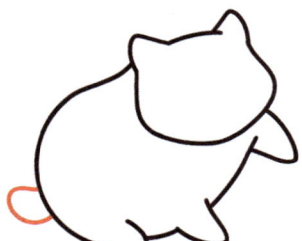

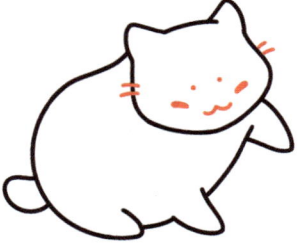

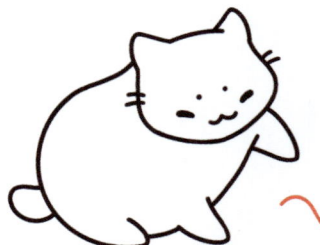

7. Add the tail.

8. Give your kitty a fun facial expression.

9. Start drawing the bird with a curved line for the top of the head and back.

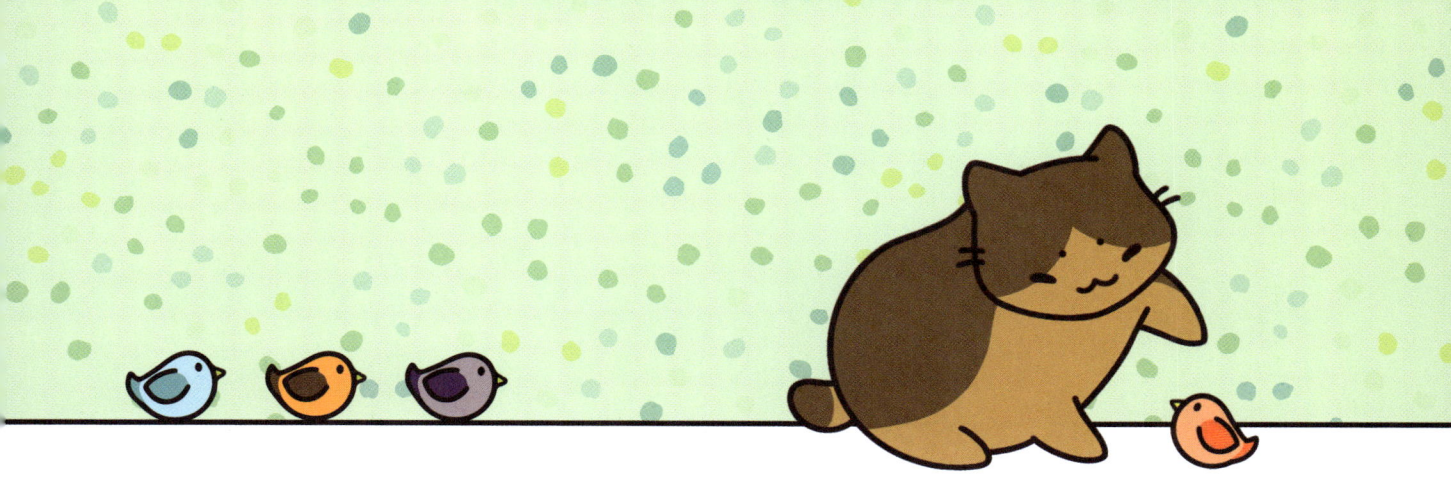

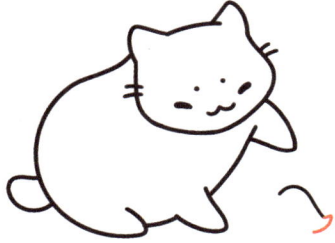

10. Give it a pointy tail.

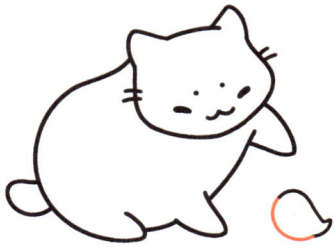

11. Draw a rotund breast.

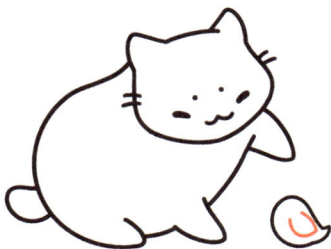

12. Add a wing.

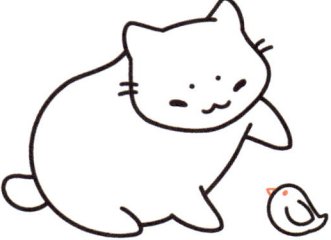

13. Finish by drawing a dot for the bird's eye, along with a pointy, little beak.

THE OBSERVER

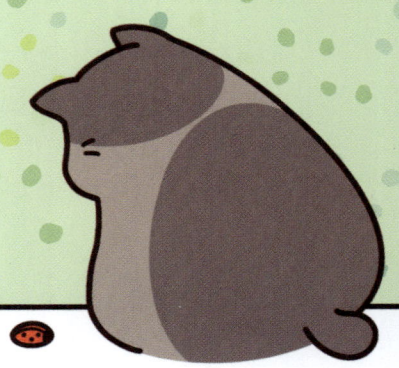

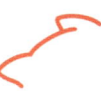

1. Draw the top of the head and the ears tilted to the left and facing downward.

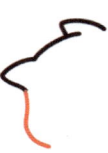

2. Draw the left side of the head.

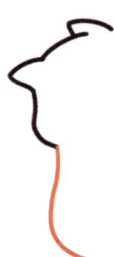

3. Draw the left side of the body.

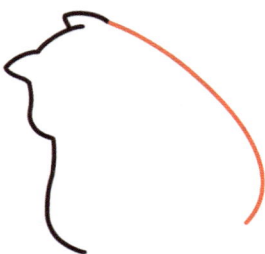

4. Draw the right side of the body.

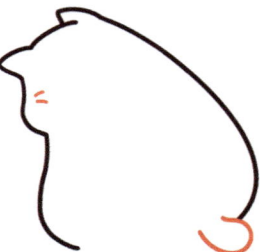

5. Add the tail and whiskers.

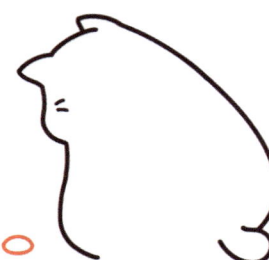

6. Draw a small oval to the left of the kitty for the ladybug.

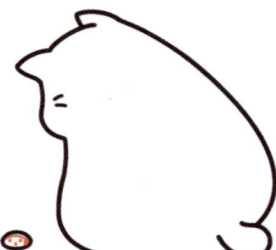

7. Finish by adding dot and stripe details to the ladybug.

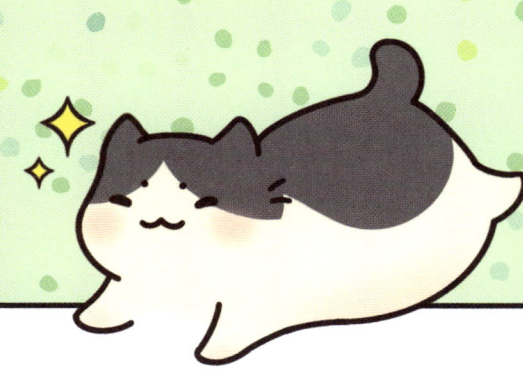

THE RUNNER

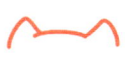

1. Draw the top of the head and the ears.

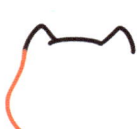

2. Draw the left side of the head.

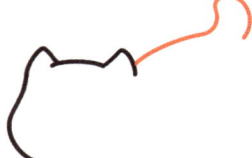

3. Draw the back of the body with the tail.

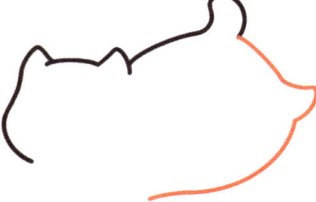

4. Draw the back leg and underside of the body, extending from the tail.

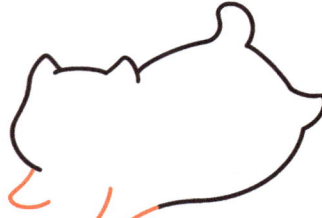

5. Draw the front legs stretched out in front of the body.

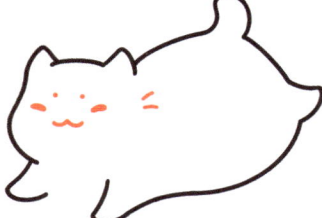

6. Give your kitty a fun facial expression.

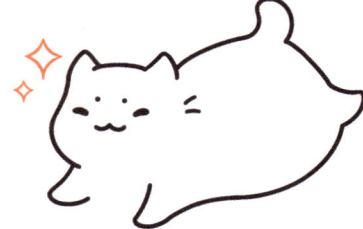

7. Finish by adding some diamond sparkles around your kitty's head.

DAILY ACTIVITIES

I wonder where this
fat came from . . .

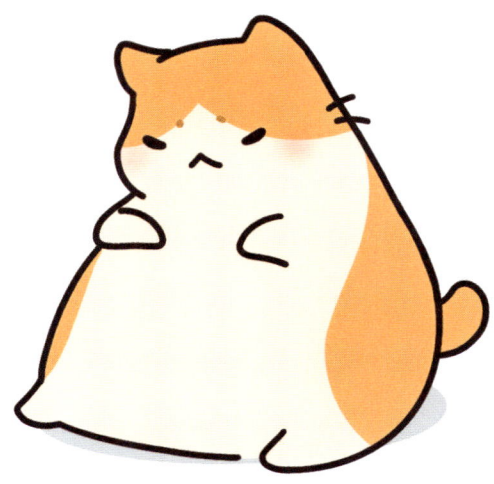

Meanwhile . . .

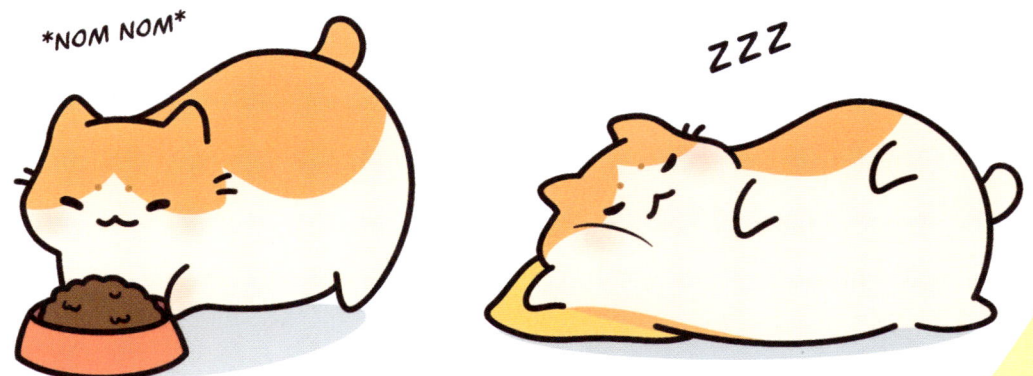

Eat. Sleep. Repeat.

THE LOUNGER

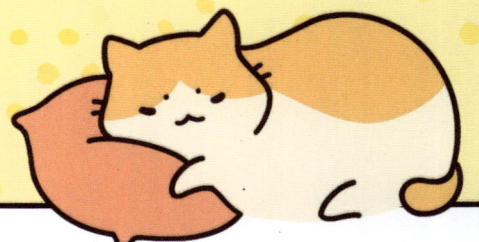

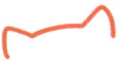

1. Draw the top of the head and the ears slightly tilted to the left.

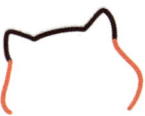

2. Draw both sides of the head.

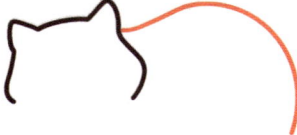

3. Draw the back of the body.

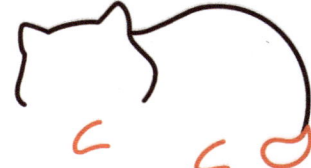

4. Add the front and back legs, along with the tail.

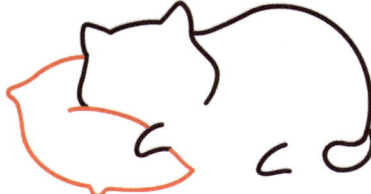

5. Draw the pillow with four curved lines, connecting them with pointy yet rounded corners.

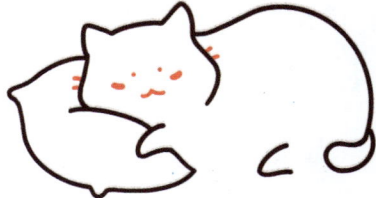

6. Finish by giving your kitty a fun facial expression.

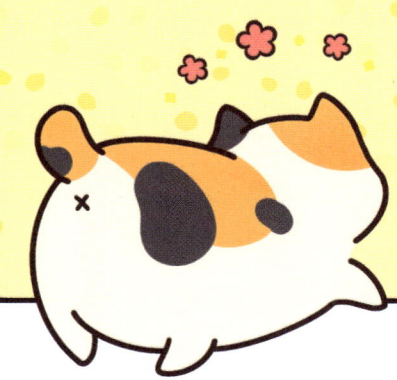

THE WANDERER

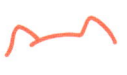

1. Draw the top of the head and the ears slightly tilted to the left.

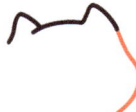

2. Draw the right side of the head.

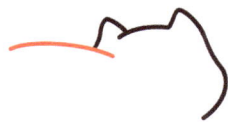

3. Draw the back of the body.

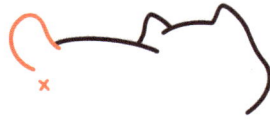

4. Add the tail and an X for, well, you know.

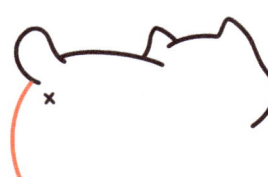

5. Draw the haunch and back leg on the left side.

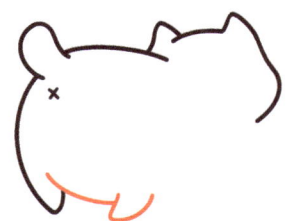

6. Draw the underside of the body and the other back leg.

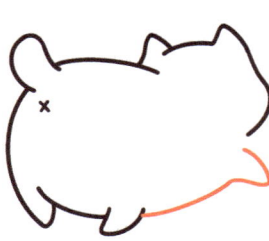

7. Continue drawing the underside of the body, extending it into the front leg.

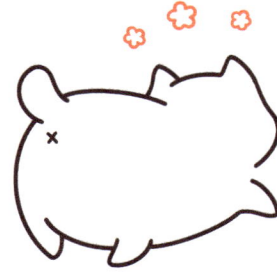

8. Finish by adding some flower details above your kitty's head.

THE GOOD EATER

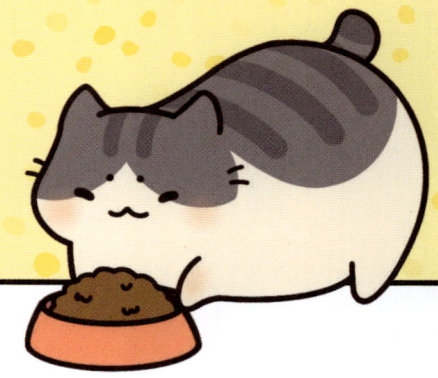

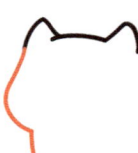

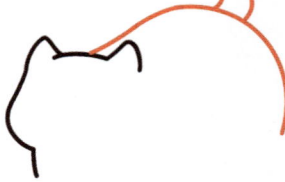

1. Draw the top of the head and the ears.

2. Draw the left side of the head, extending the line into the leg.

3. Draw the back of the body. Add the tail.

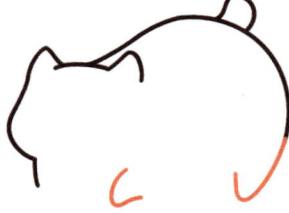

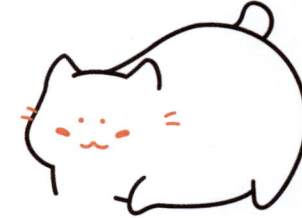

4. Draw the front and back legs.

5. Draw the underside of the body.

6. Give your kitty a fun facial expression.

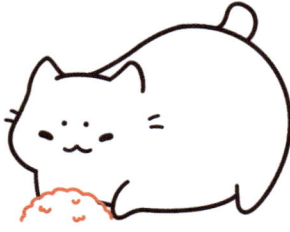

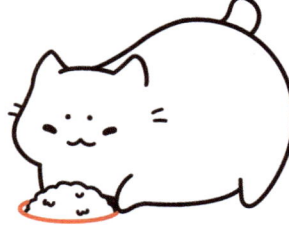

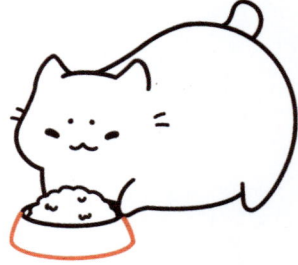

7. Draw a mound of yummy food.

8. Draw a semicircle around the food for the top of the bowl.

9. Finish by drawing the base and sides of the bowl, making the base wider than the top.

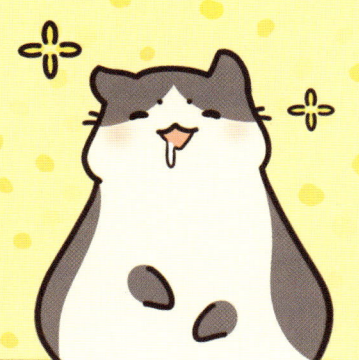

THE DAYDREAMER

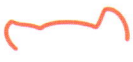

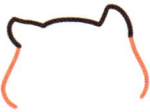

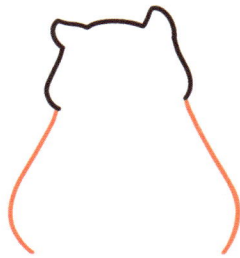

1. Draw the top of the head and the ears, with the ear on the left side being a little droopy.

2. Draw the sides of the head.

3. Draw the sides of the body.

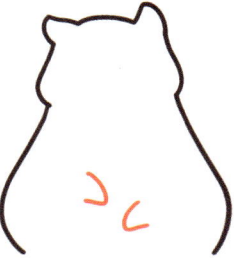

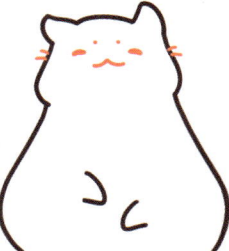

4. Draw the front legs slightly askew.

5. Give your kitty a fun facial expression.

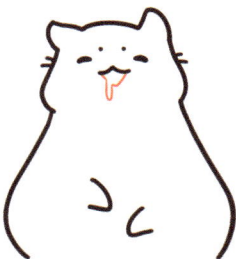

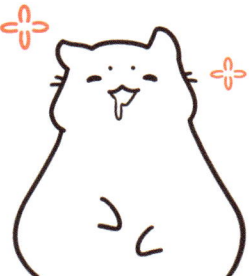

6. Add some drool dripping from the mouth.

7. Finish by adding a couple of starbursts around your kitty.

THE ROLLER-AROUNDER

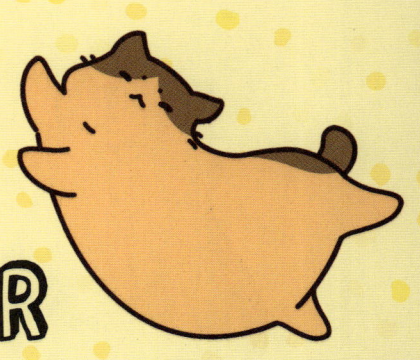

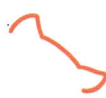

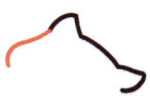

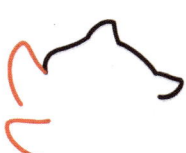

1. Draw the top of the head and the ears tilted to the right.

2. Draw the left side of the head.

3. Draw the front legs so they're raised and splayed apart.

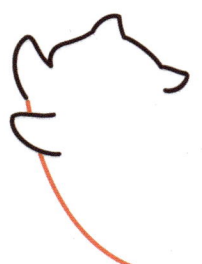

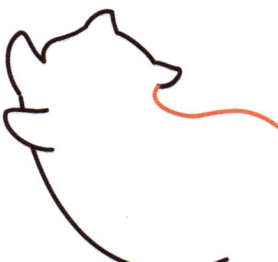

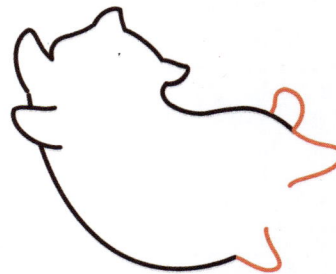

4. Draw the front of the body.

5. Draw the back of the body, giving it a little more curve.

6. Add the back legs, also splayed apart, along with the tail.

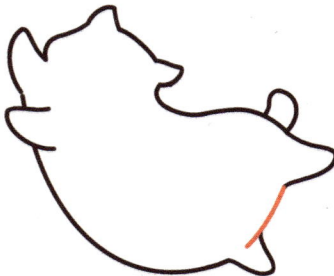

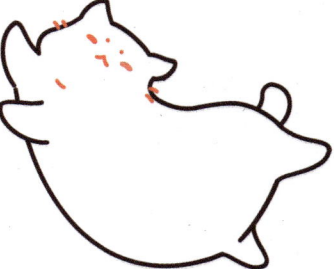

7. Draw the underside of the body between the back legs.

8. Finish by giving your kitty a fun facial expression.

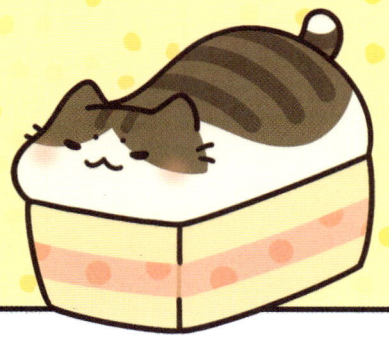

THE BOX TESTER

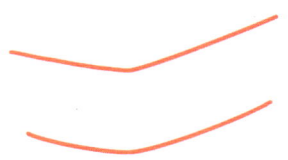

1. Starting with the box, draw two angled, parallel lines.

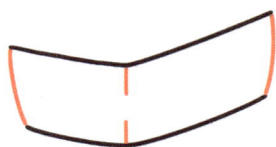

2. Connect the top and bottom lines at the three edges with slightly curved lines.

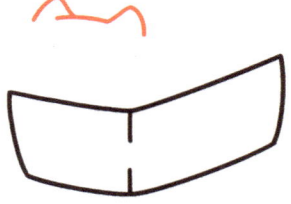

3. Draw the top of the head and the ears of your kitty slightly tilted to the right.

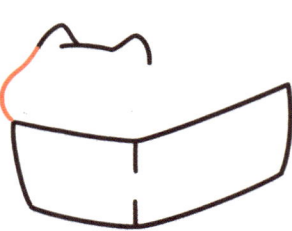

4. Draw the left side of the head.

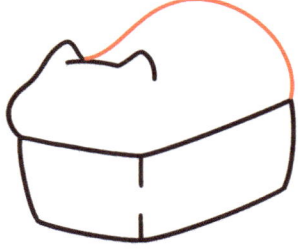

5. Draw the back of the body.

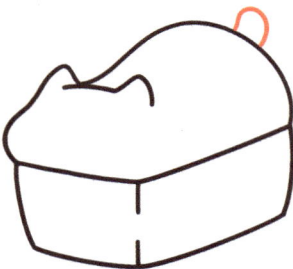

6. Add the tail.

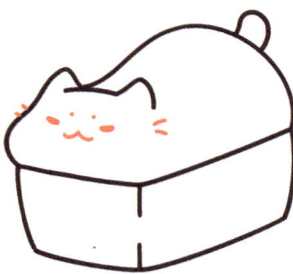

7. Give your kitty a fun facial expression.

THE STRUTTER

1. Draw the top of the head and the ears tilted to the right.

2. Draw the left side of the head.

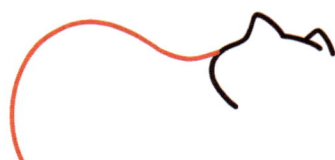

3. Draw the back of the body.

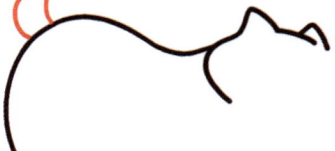

4. Add the tail.

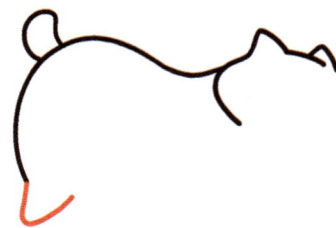

5. Draw the outer-back leg.

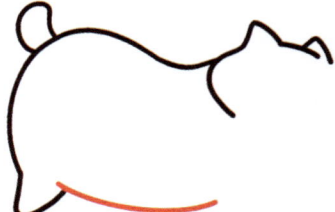

6. Draw the underside of the body.

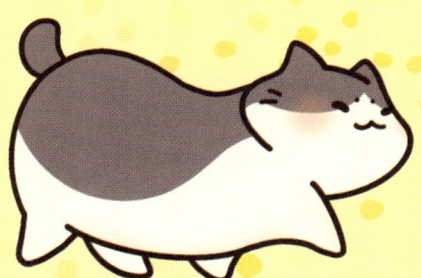

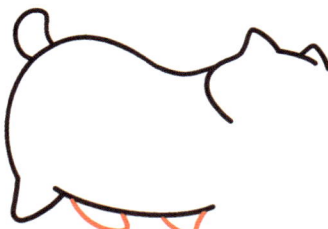

7. Draw the inner-front and -back legs.

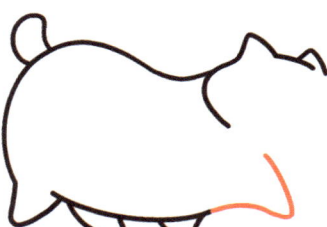

8. Draw the outer-front leg lifted up as if walking.

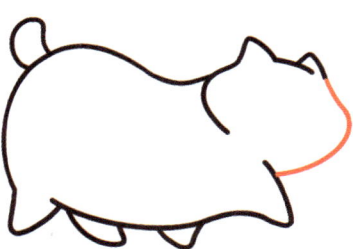

9. Draw the right side of the head.

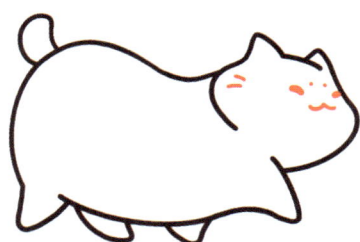

10. Finish by giving your kitty a fun facial expression.

THE CRYBABY

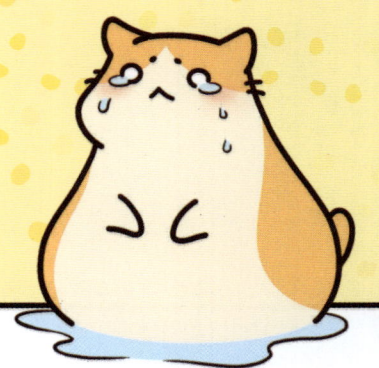

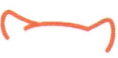

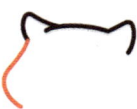

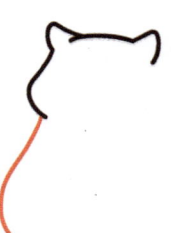

1. Draw the top of the head and the ears slightly tilted to the right.

2. Draw the left side of the head.

3. Draw the left side of the body.

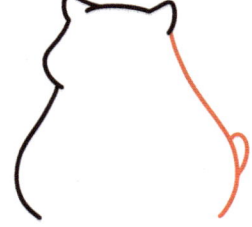

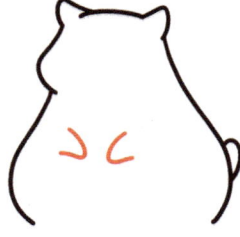

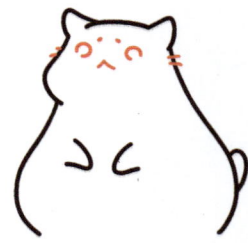

4. Draw the right side of the body. Add the tail.

5. Draw the front legs, facing each other, in the center of the body.

6. Give your kitty a sad face.

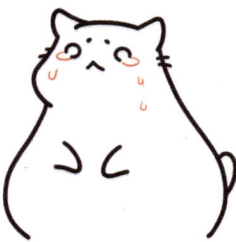

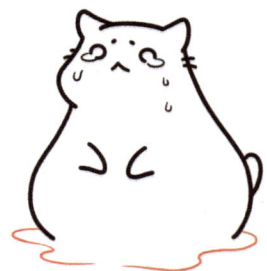

7. Add lots of tears.

8. Finish by adding a puddle of tears all around your kitty.

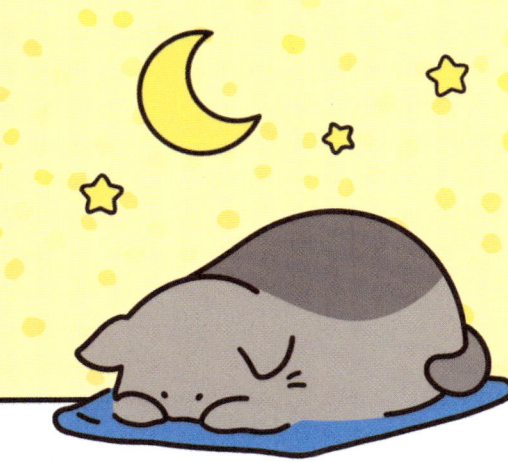

THE SNOOZER

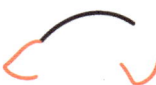

1. Draw the top of the head slightly tilted to the left.

2. Draw the ears so that they're facing downward.

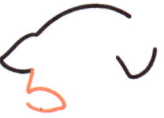

3. Draw the front leg on the left side of the face as if it's covering the eye.

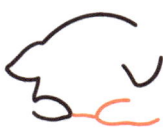

4. Draw the other front leg in the same way. Connect them with a line.

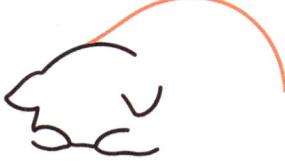

5. Draw the back of the body.

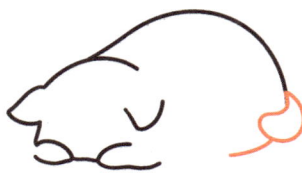

6. Add the tail. Extend a line from the tail for the underside of the body.

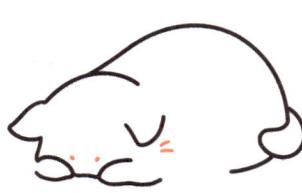

7. Add the eyebrows and whiskers.

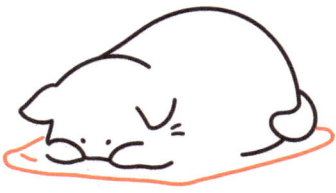

8. Draw the shape of the blanket around the kitty.

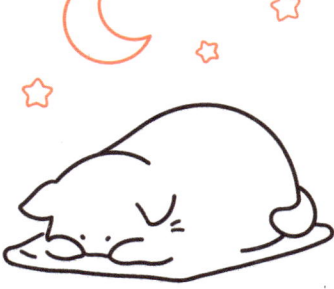

9. Finish with a moon and stars above your kitty for sweet dreams.

THE SHOW-OFF

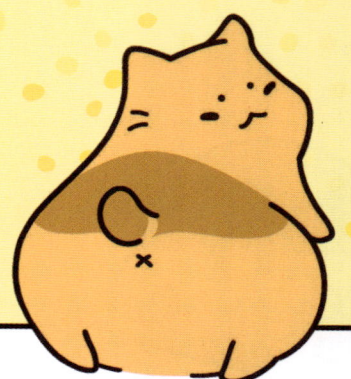

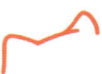

1. Draw the top of the head and the ears tilted to the left.

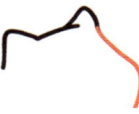

2. Draw the right side of the head.

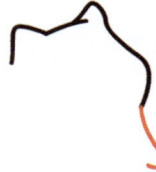

3. Extend the front leg from the right side of the head.

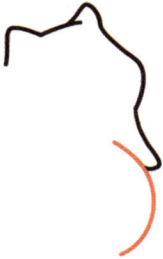

4. Draw the right side of the body.

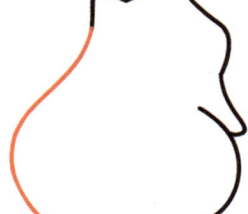

5. Draw the left side of body.

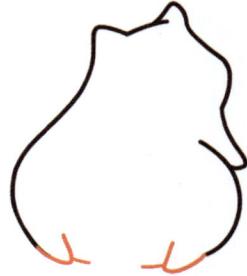

6. Add the back legs with short lines extending from each one.

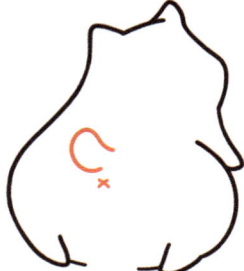

7. Add the tail, along with an X for, well, you know.

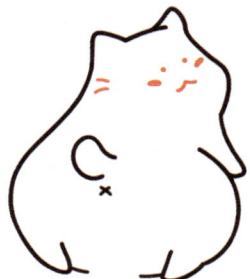

8. Finish by giving your kitty a fun facial expression.

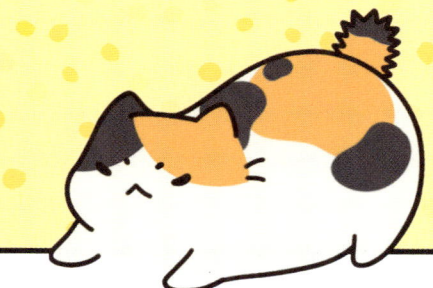

THE TROUBLEMAKER

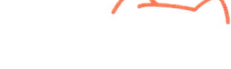

1. Draw the top of the head and the ears slightly tilted to the right.

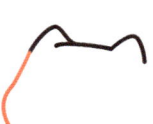

2. Draw the left side of the head.

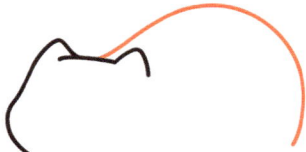

3. Draw the back of the body.

· ·

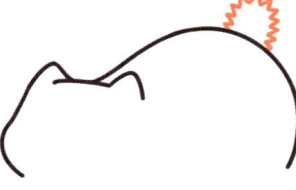

4. Add the tail, giving it jagged edges to express this kitty's irritation!

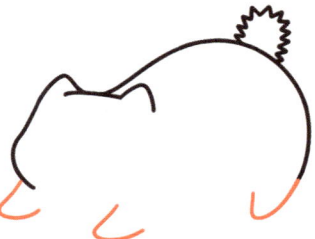

5. Draw the three legs.

· ·

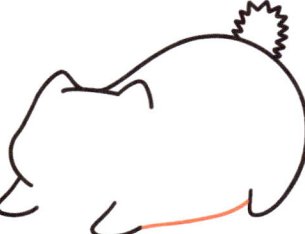

6. Draw the underside of the body.

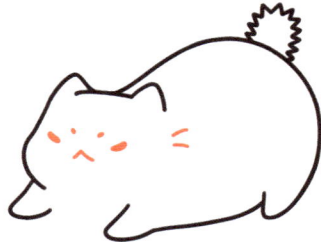

7. Finish by giving your kitty an irritated face.

THE SNACKER

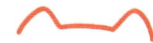

1. Draw the top of the head and the ears.

2. Extend lines from the ears for the upper half of the head.

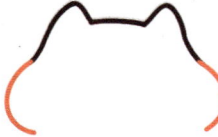

3. Draw the remaining sides of the head with large curves for chubby cheeks.

4. Give your kitty a fun facial expression.

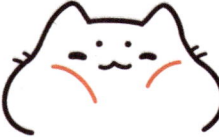

5. Add curved lines to the face to define those chubby cheeks even more.

6. Draw the sides of the body.

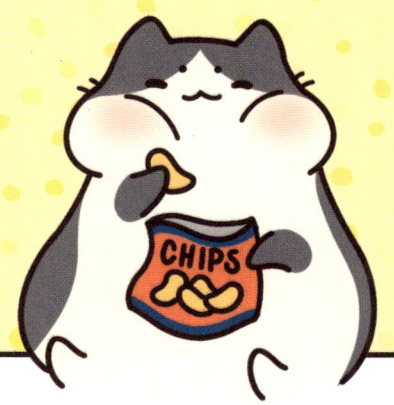

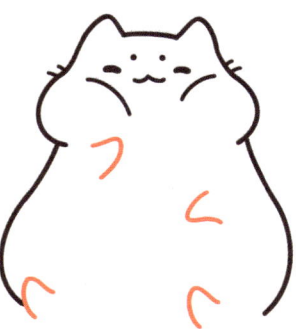

7. Draw the front legs with the one on the right side lower to hold the bag of chips and the one on the left side closer to the face to hold a chip. Add the back legs so they're sticking up.

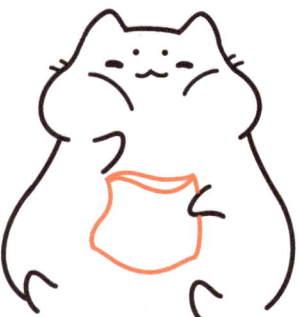

8. Position the bag of chips so it's "held" by the lower-front leg. Draw the bag as a rectangle with curved sides. Add a second line across the top to give it depth.

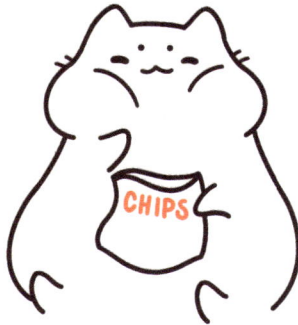

9. Write the word "CHIPS" on the bag.

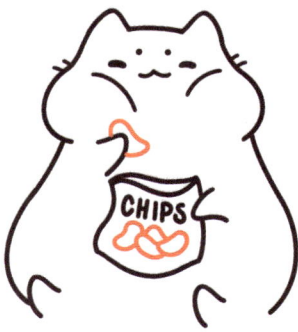

10. Finish by placing a chip in the upper-front leg and decorating the bag with images of chips.

THE BELLY FLOPPER

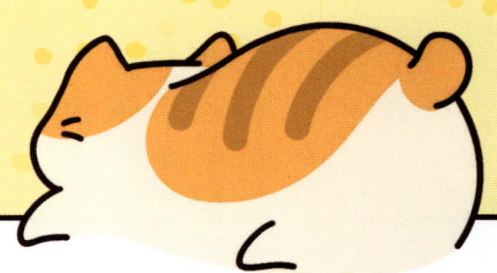

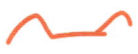

1. Draw the top of the head and the ears, making the ear on the right side incomplete.

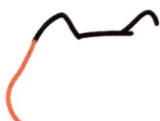

2. Draw the left side of the head.

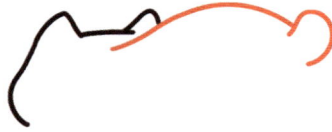

3. Draw the back of the body with the tail.

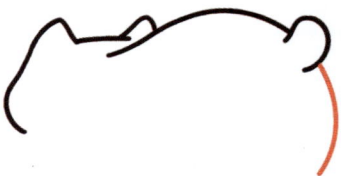

4. Continue drawing the back of the body, extending it from the tail.

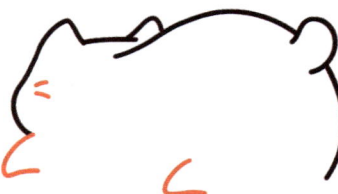

5. Finish by adding the front and back legs to your kitty, along with its whiskers.

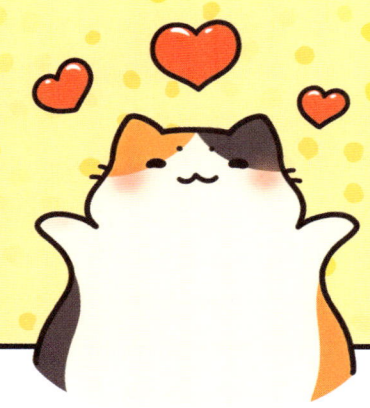

THE LOVER

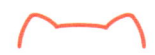

1. Draw the top of the head and the ears.

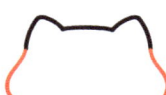

2. Draw the sides of the head.

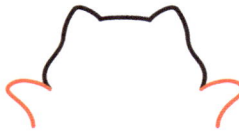

3. Draw the front legs raised up next to the head.

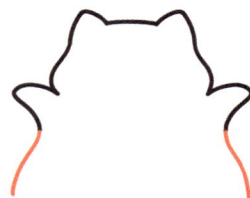

4. Draw the sides of the body.

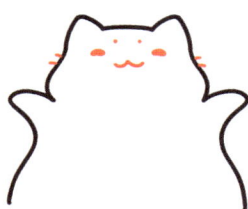

5. Give your kitty a fun facial expression.

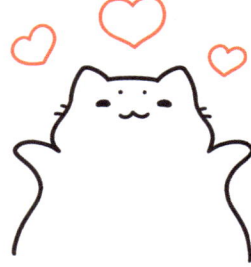

6. Finish by adding hearts around your kitty.

THE GIVER

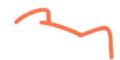

1. Draw the top of the head and the ears tilted to the right.

2. Draw the left side of the head.

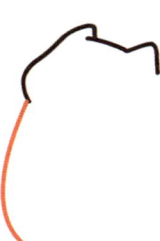

3. Draw the left side of the body.

4. Draw the back of the body.

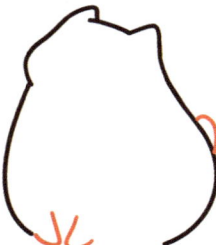

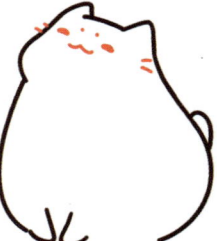

5. Position the front legs together closer to the left side of the body. Add the tail.

6. Give your kitty a fun facial expression.

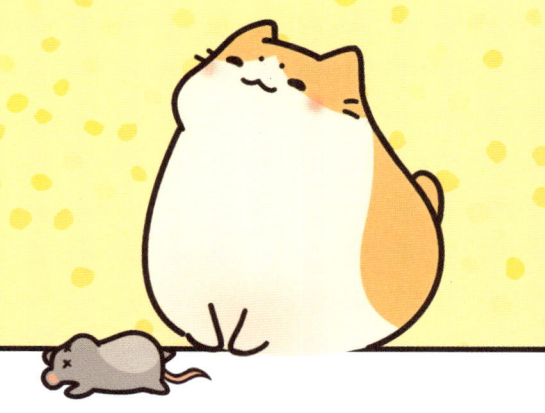

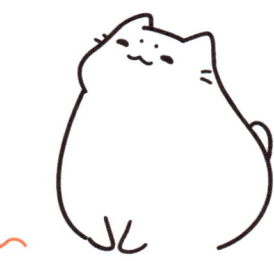

7. Start drawing the mouse with a curved line for the head.

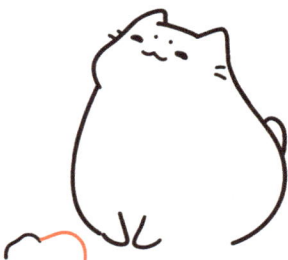

8. Continue drawing the front of the mouse's body.

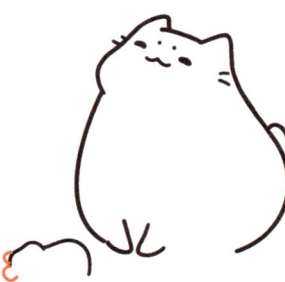

9. Add the ears.

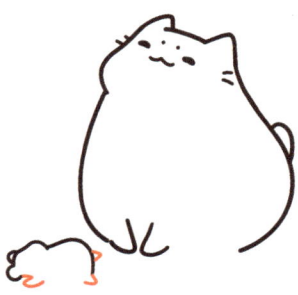

10. Draw three little feet.

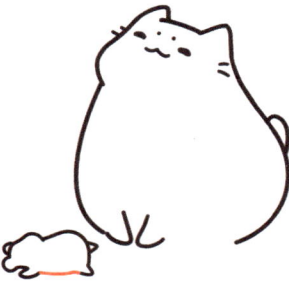

11. Draw the back of the body.

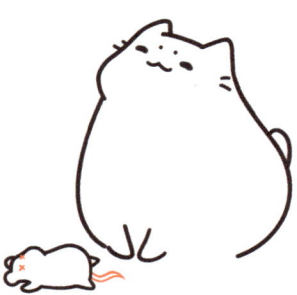

12. Finish by drawing little Xs for the mouse's eyes, along with the tail.

THE GRUMP

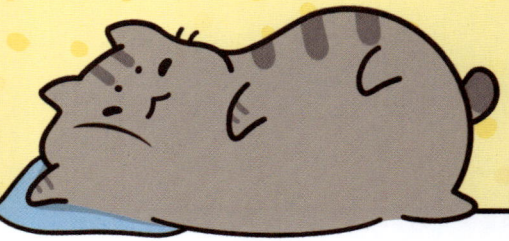

1. Draw the top of the head and the ears tilted to the left.

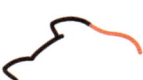

2. Draw the right side of the head.

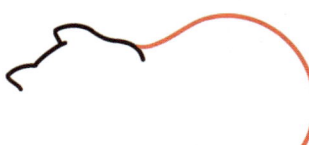

3. Draw the upper side of the body.

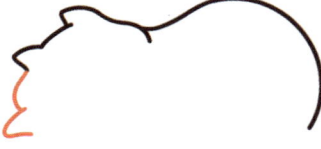

4. Draw the left side of the face a bit wider, with the lower-front leg extending from it.

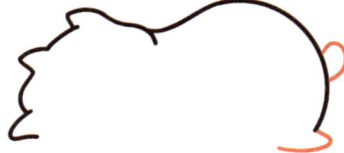

5. Add the tail, along with the lower-back leg.

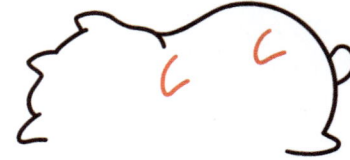

6. Draw the upper-front and -back legs on the body.

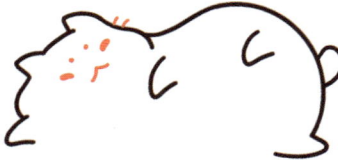

7. Give your kitty a fun facial expression.

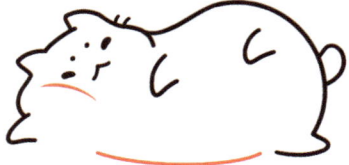

8. Draw the lower side of the body. Add a curved line to the face to define that it's a bit smooshed.

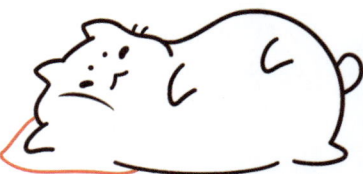

9. Finish by adding a comfy pillow for your kitty to rest its head on.

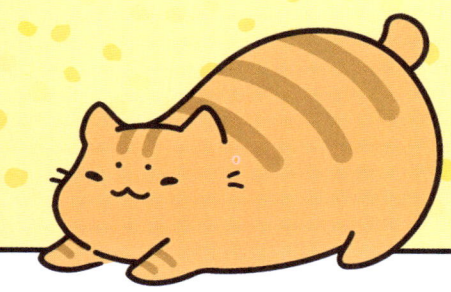

THE STRETCHER

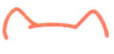

1. Draw the top of the head and the ears.

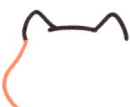

2. Draw the left side of the head.

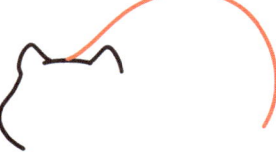

3. Draw the back of the body.

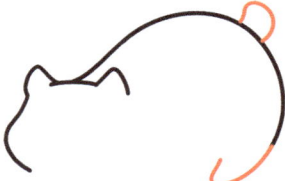

4. Extend the body into the back leg. Add the tail.

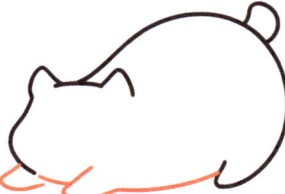

5. Draw the underside of the body, extending it into the outer-front leg. Add the inner-front leg.

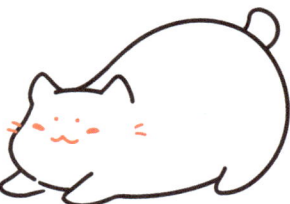

6. Finish by giving your kitty a fun facial expression.

THE DOZER

1. Starting with the box, draw a rectangle.

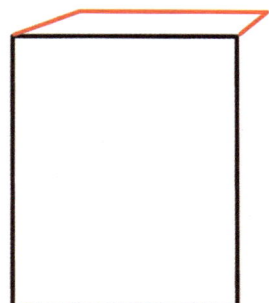

2. Draw the top of the box, placing the lines at slight angles.

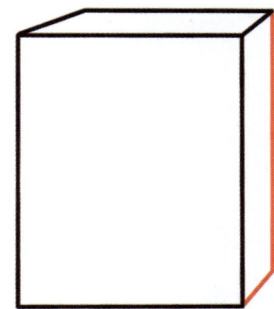

3. Draw the side of the box, making the base line slightly angled.

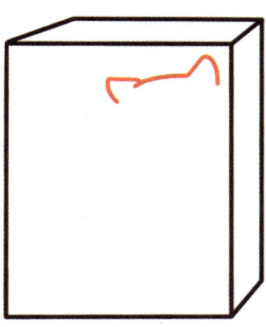

4. Draw the top of the kitty's head and the ears tilted to the left.

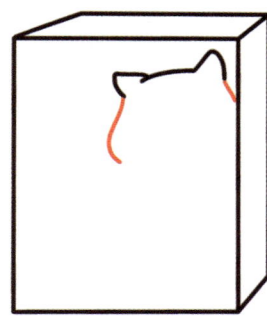

5. Draw the left side of the head and part of the right side.

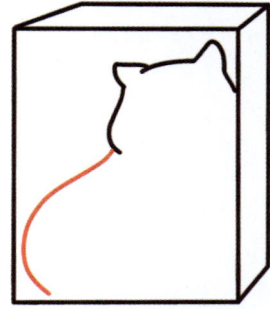

6. Draw the left side of the body.

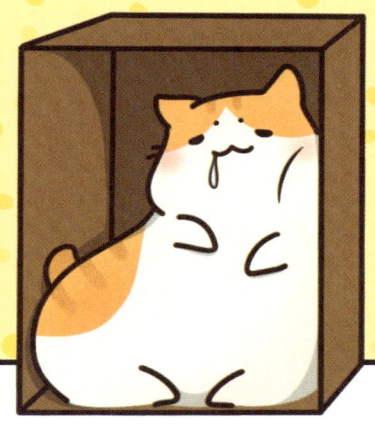

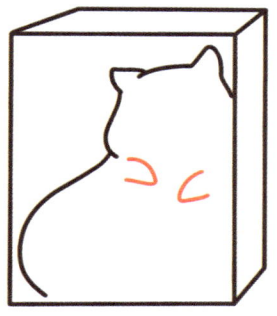

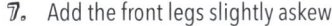

7. Add the front legs slightly askew.

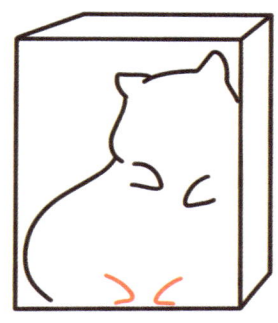

8. Draw the back legs so they're facing each other.

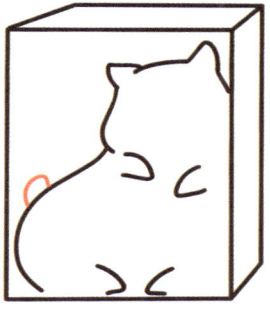

9. Add the tail.

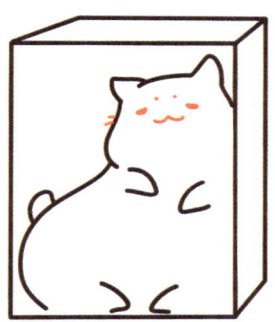

10. Give your kitty a fun facial expression.

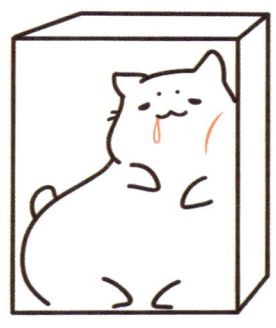

11. Draw a large drop of drool. Add a curved line to the right side of the face to define that it's a bit smooshed.

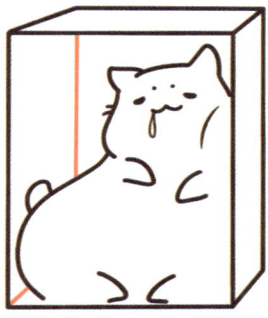

12. Finish by drawing the left side of the box.

BEING CURIOUS

Don't be afraid of the darkness.

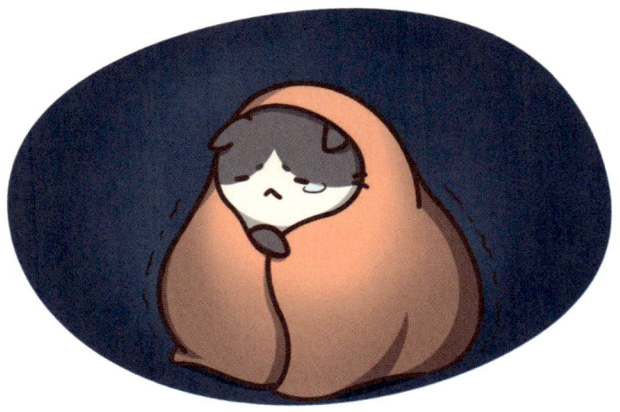

That's when stars shine brightest.

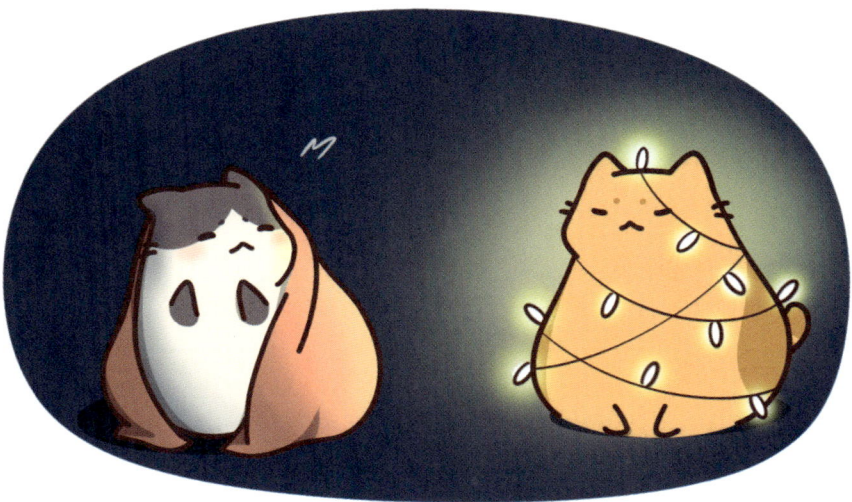

THE EXPLORER

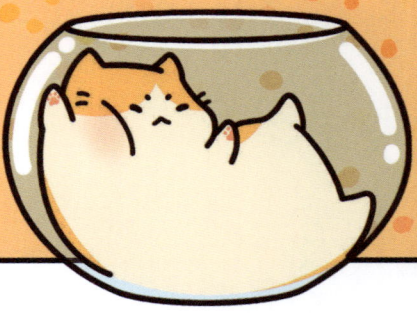

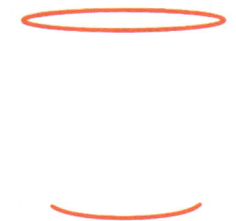

1. Starting with the fishbowl, draw a narrow oval for the top of the bowl and a curved line, smaller than the oval, for the base of the bowl.

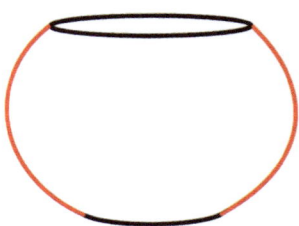

2. Connect the two shapes with convex lines.

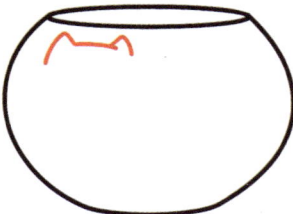

3. Draw the top of the head and the ears of your kitty in the upper-left side of the fishbowl.

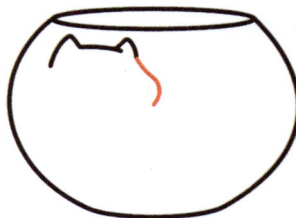

4. Draw the right side of the head.

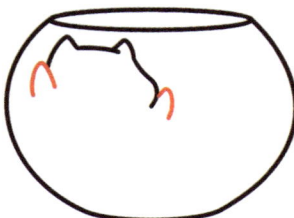

5. Add the front legs raised up by the sides of the head.

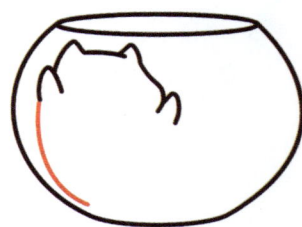

6. Draw the back of the body.

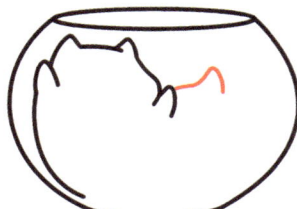

7. Draw the front of the body with the back leg extending from it.

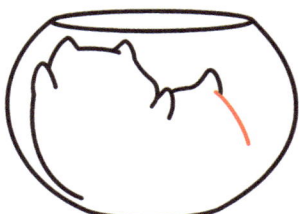

8. Draw the underside of the body, extending from the back leg.

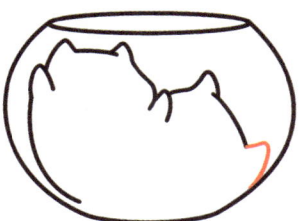

9. Draw the other back leg.

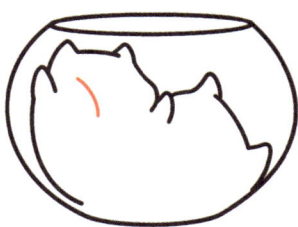

10. Add a curved line to the left side of the face to show that your kitty is smooshed against the glass.

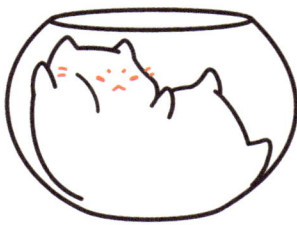

11. Give your kitty a fun facial expression.

THE NATURE LOVER

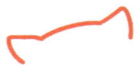

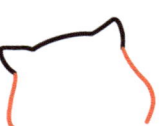

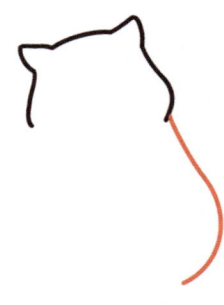

1. Draw the top of the head and the ears tilted to the left.

2. Draw both sides of the head.

3. Draw the right side of the body.

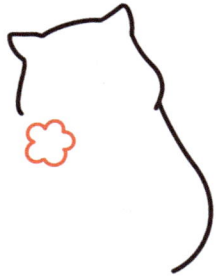

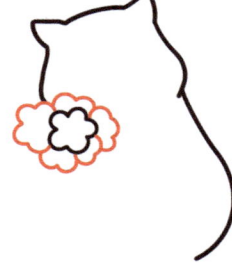

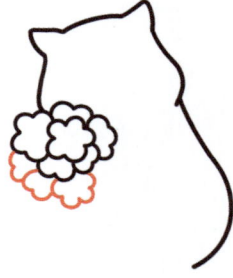

4. Add a flower shape to the left side of the body, directly below the head.

5. Make a bouquet by adding more flowers around the one you just drew.

6. Make the bouquet even larger!

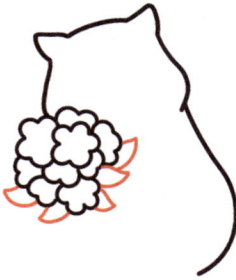

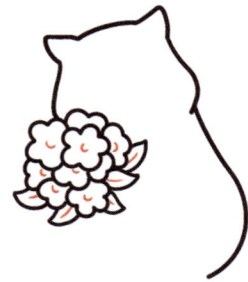

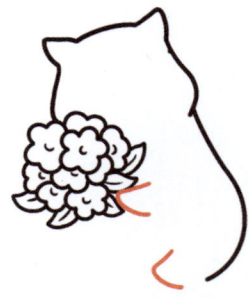

7. Add leaves as V shapes to the base of the bouquet.

8. Give the flowers and leaves some details with curved lines.

9. Draw the front and back legs on the right side of the body.

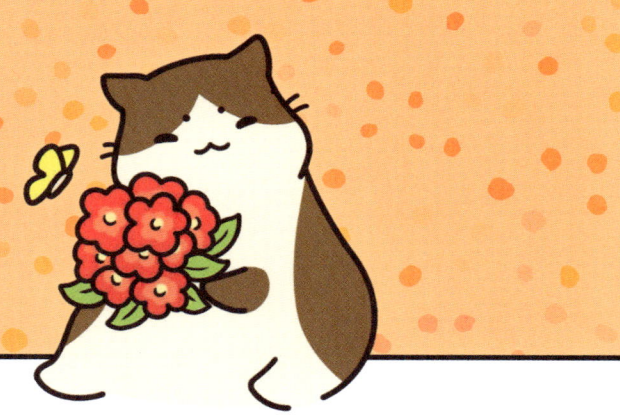

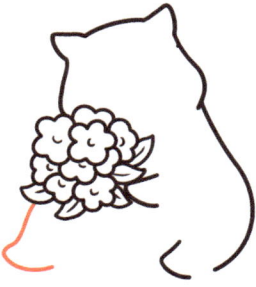

10. Draw the left side of the body below the bouquet, extending it into the back leg.

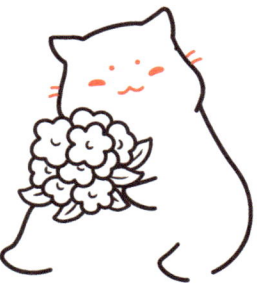

11. Give your kitty a fun facial expression.

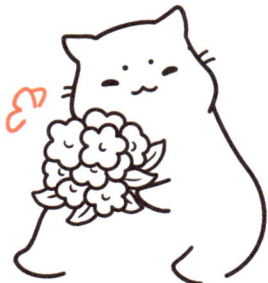

12. Add the butterfly to the left of your kitty by drawing the wings.

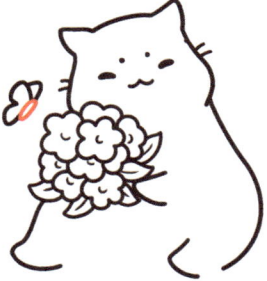

13. Finish by drawing a small oval for the butterfly's body.

THE INVESTIGATOR

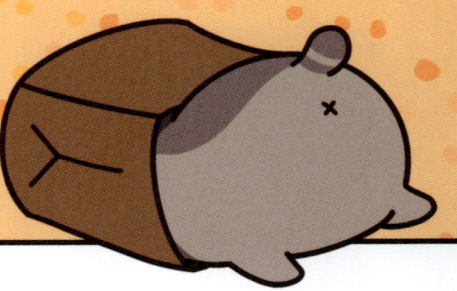

1. Start with the tail and an X for, well, you know.

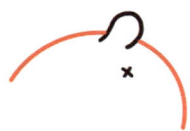

2. Draw the haunches of the body, extending from each side of the tail.

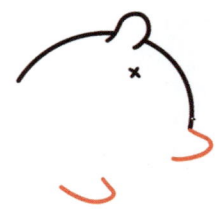

3. Draw the back legs.

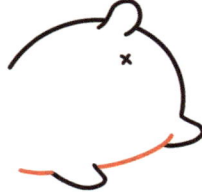

4. Draw the underside of the body.

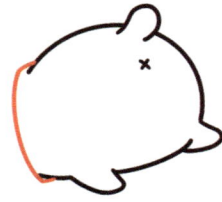

5. Draw a slightly curved line around your kitty's body for the opening of the bag.

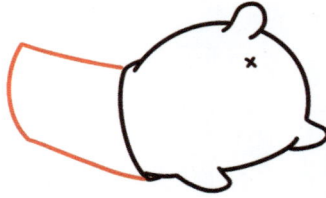

6. Continue drawing the bag with three slightly curved lines for the left side.

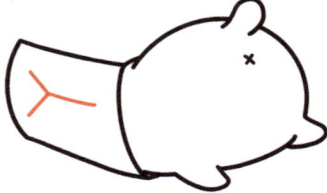

7. Add a Y shape to the side of the bag to define its folds.

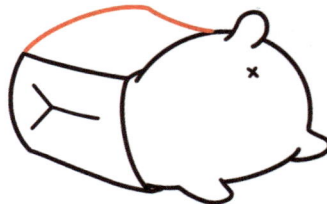

8. Finish by drawing two more slightly curved lines for the top and right side of the bag.

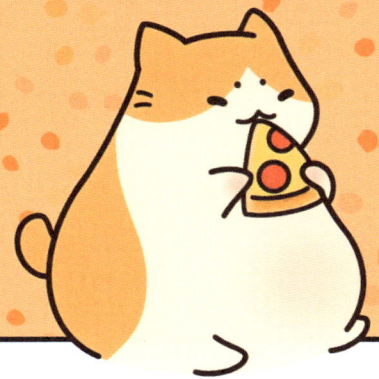

THE FOODIE

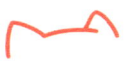

1. Draw the top of the head and the ears slightly tilted to the left.

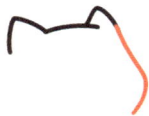

2. Draw the right side of the head.

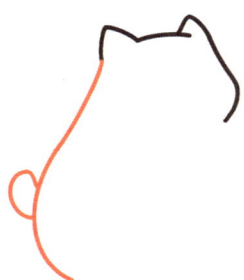

3. Draw the back of the body. Add the tail.

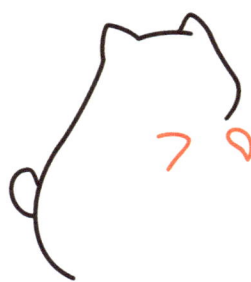

4. Draw the front legs so they can "hold" the slice of pizza.

5. Draw the front of the body, along with the back legs.

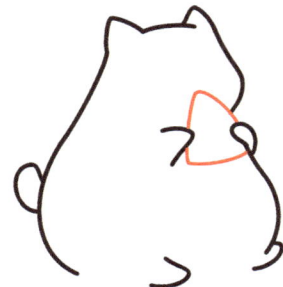

6. Draw the slice of pizza as a triangle between the front legs.

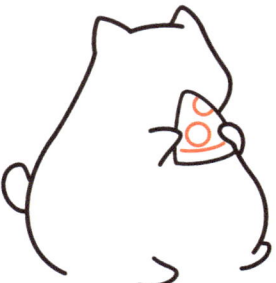

7. Add your favorite toppings!

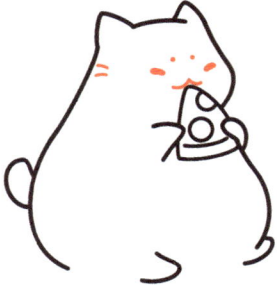

8. Finish by giving your kitty a fun facial expression.

THE STUDENT

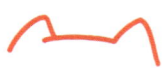

1. Draw the head and the ears.

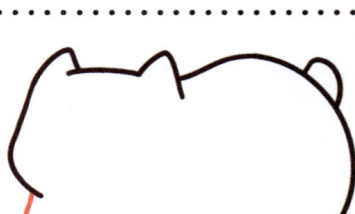

2. Draw the left side of the head.

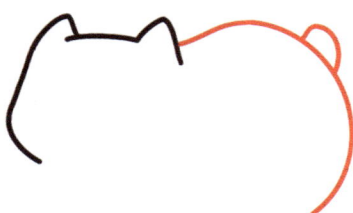

3. Draw the back of the body. Add the tail.

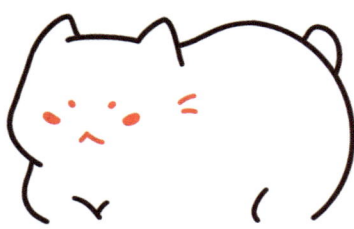

4. Draw the left side of the body. Add short curved lines to show that the legs are tucked under the body.

5. Give your kitty a fun facial expression.

6. Draw one side of the book "underneath" your kitty with three slightly curved lines.

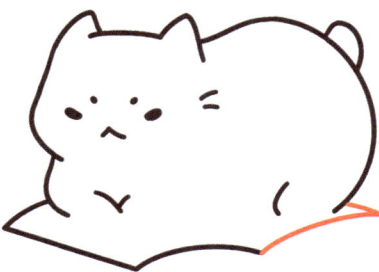

7. Draw the other side of the book with two more slightly curved lines.

8. Draw an L shape around the book to give it depth. Don't forget the notch in the center for the spine.

9. Connect the shapes at the corners with short, curved lines.

10. Finish by adding lines to the book to show texture for the pages.

THE SPELUNKER

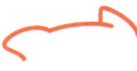

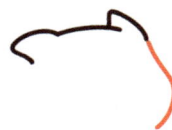

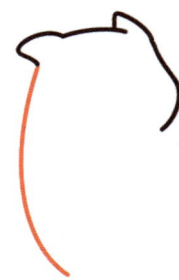

1. Draw the top of the head and the ears, with the ear on the left bent back a bit more.

2. Draw the right side of the head.

3. Draw the left side of the head and body.

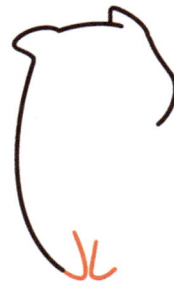

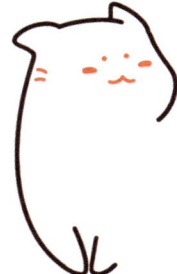

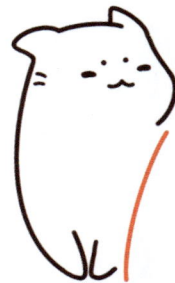

4. Position the front pegs together in front of the body.

5. Give your kitty a fun facial expression.

6. Draw a slanted line along the right side of your kitty for the edge of the blanket.

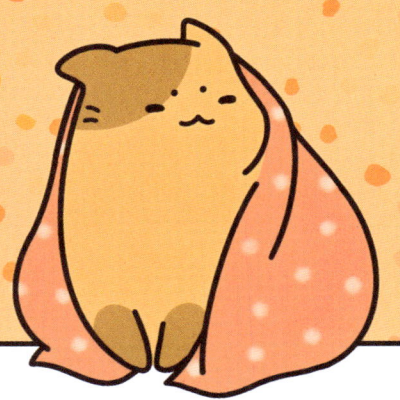

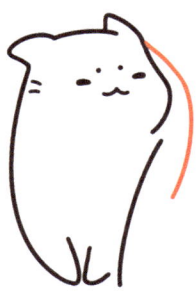

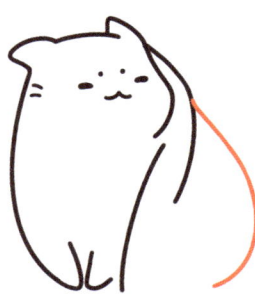

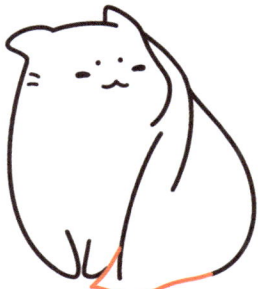

7. Add a curved line to the right of the head for the fold in the blanket.

8. Draw the back of the body, though it is covered in the blanket.

9. Complete the right side of the blanket with lines that meet at a point at the bottom.

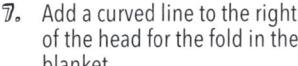

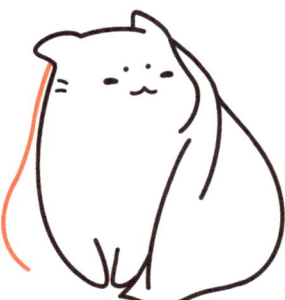

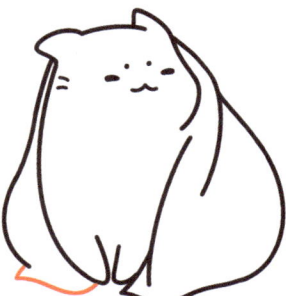

10. Continue drawing the blanket on the left side, with a curved line extending from the ear down the length of the body.

11. Finish by drawing the bottom edge of the blanket.

THE FISHER

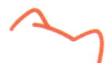

1. Draw the top of the head and the ears tilted to the right.

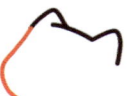

2. Draw the left side of the head.

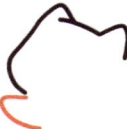

3. Draw the front leg directly below the head.

4. Draw the underside of the body, with the line starting above the leg and then extending below it.

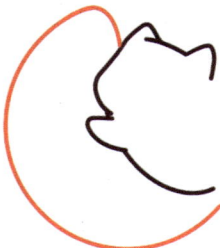

5. Draw a crescent-moon shape to the left of your kitty for the body of the fish.

6. Draw two curved lines at the base of the fish's body for the tail fin.

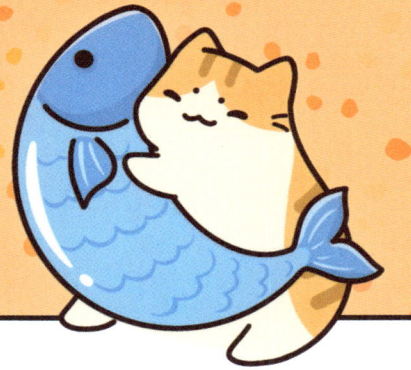

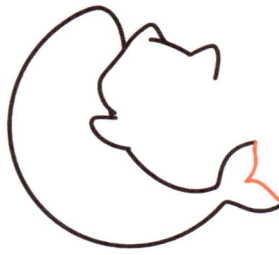

7. Draw two more curved lines to complete the tail fin.

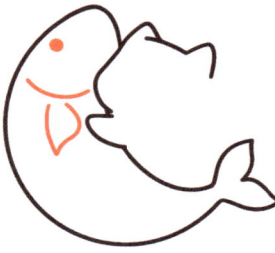

8. Complete the fish with a circle for the eye, a curved line for the gill, and a curved V shape for the fin.

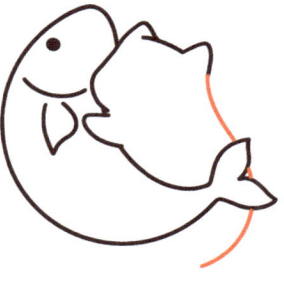

9. Draw the back of your kitty's body.

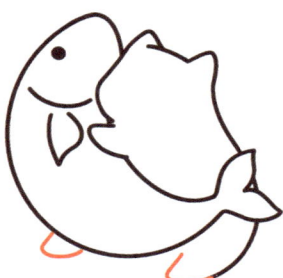

10. Add the back legs below the fish.

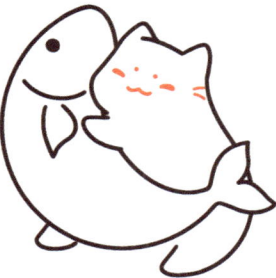

11. Give your kitty a fun facial expression.

PLAYING DRESS-UP

I thought my Halloween
costume was annoying . . .

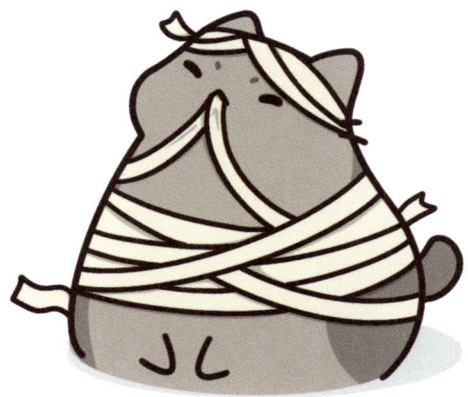

. . . until I saw that.

NICE COSTUME

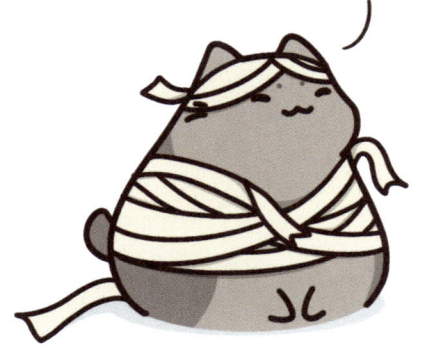

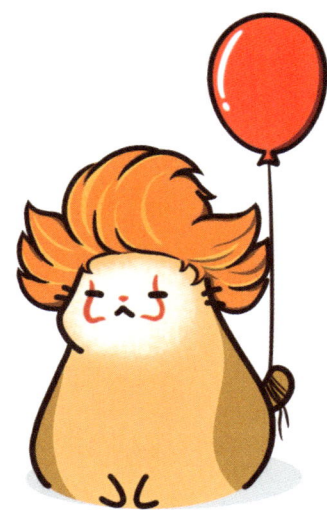

THE CATOSAURUS

1. Start by drawing the pointy horn that will sit on the top of your kitty's head.

2. Close the base of the horn with a slightly curved line.

3. Draw the top of your kitty's head with curved lines extending from both sides of the horn.

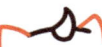

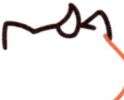

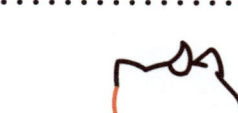

4. Add the ears.

5. Draw the right side of the head.

6. Draw the left side of the head.

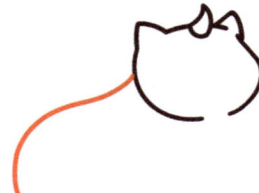

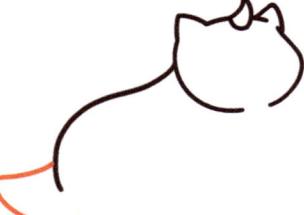

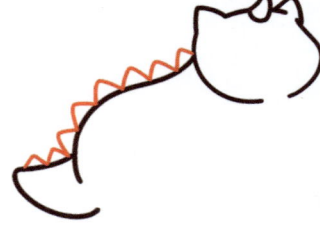

7. Draw the back of the body.

8. Add the tail—a dinosaur's tail!

9. Draw eight scales along the back and tail as upside-down V shapes.

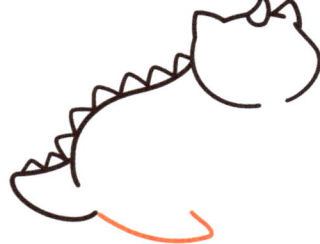

10. Draw the haunch and back leg.

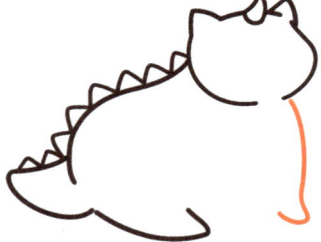

11. Draw the front of the body, extending it into the front leg.

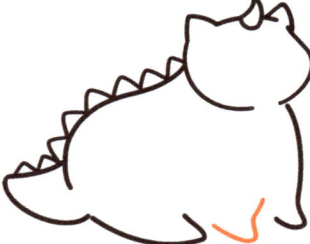

12. Add the other front leg.

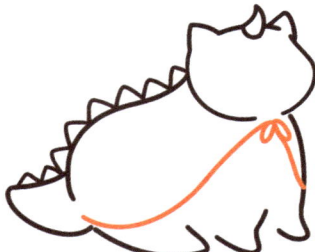

13. Draw a line that curves up the left side of the body and then curves down the right side for the costume's outline. Add loops for the tie closure.

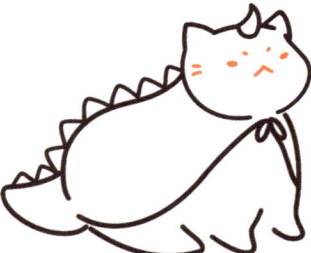

14. Finish by giving your kitty a fun facial expression.

THE BUNNY KITTY

1. Start by drawing the bunny ears.

2. Draw the sides of the headpiece.

3. Add a curved line to the headpiece to define it and give it depth.

4. Draw the right side of your kitty's head.

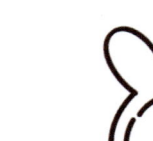

5. Add another curved line to the left side of the headpiece to define it and give it depth.

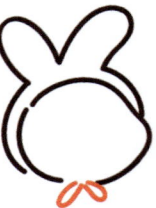

6. Add loops for the tie closure.

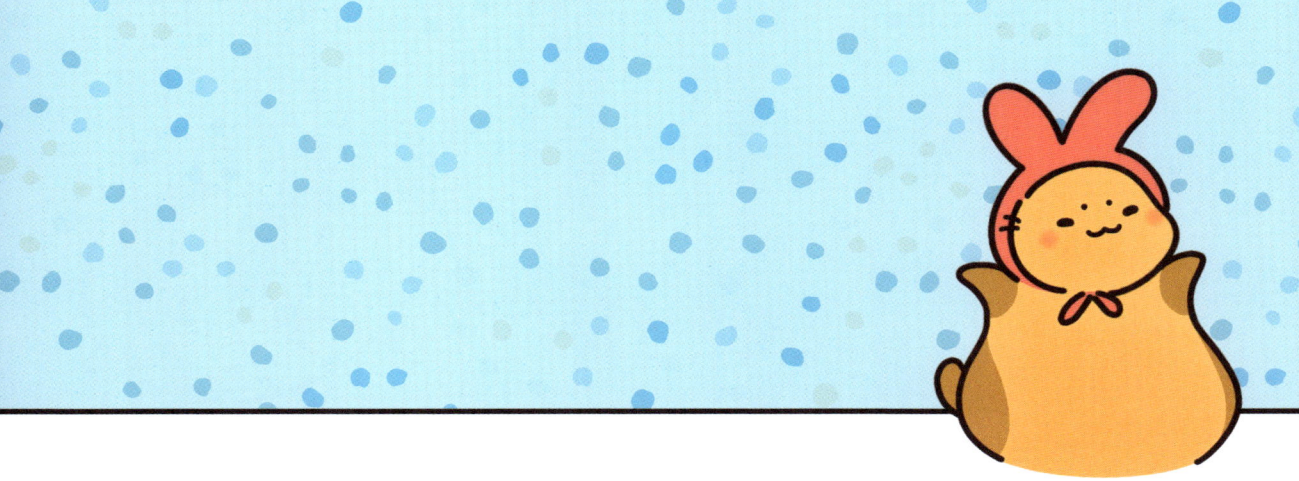

7. Draw your kitty's front legs raised up next to the head.

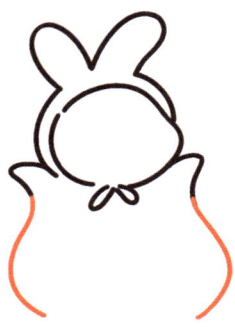

8. Draw the sides of the body.

9. Add the tail.

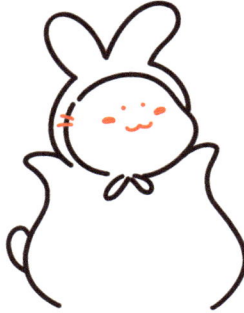

10. Finish by giving your kitty a fun facial expression.

THE BUMBLE CAT

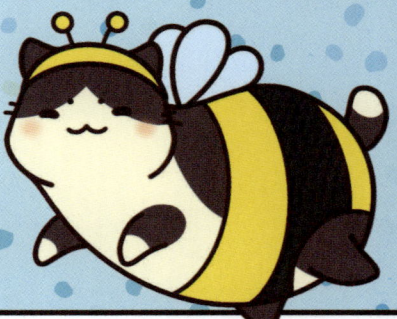

1. Start by drawing the headband for the antennas like a thin crescent moon.

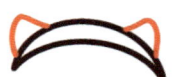

2. Draw the ears "behind" the headband.

3. Draw the antennas as lines slightly curving to the left and right with circles on top.

4. Draw the left side of the head.

5. Draw the right side of the head.

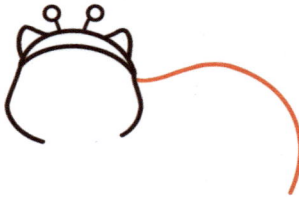

6. Draw the back of the body.

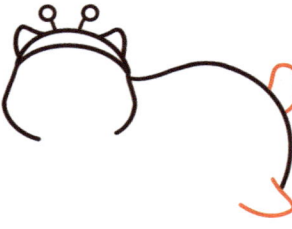

7. Add the back leg, along with the tail.

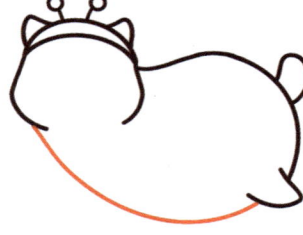

8. Draw the underside of the body.

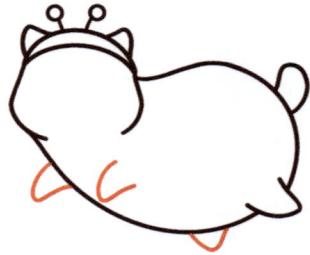

9. Draw the other three legs.

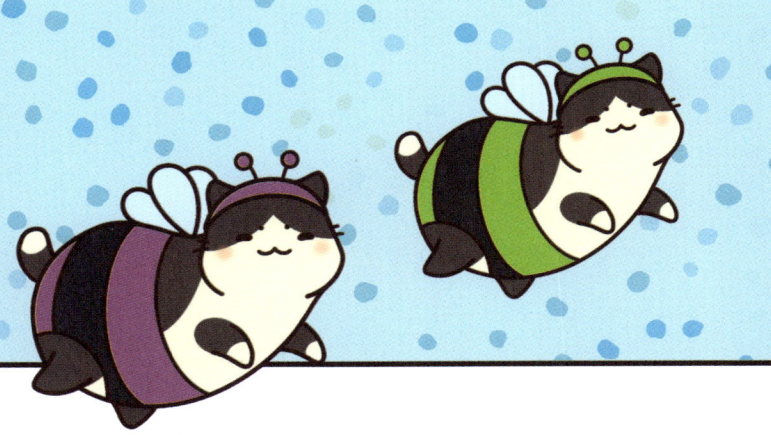

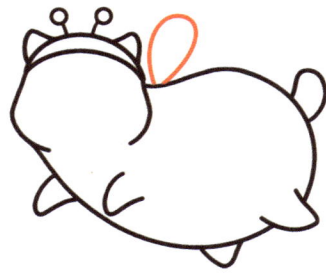

10. Draw the center wing of the bee costume as a loop.

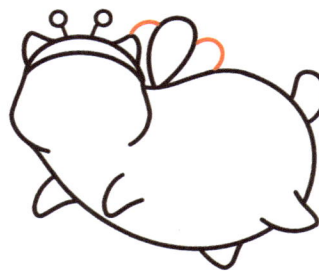

11. Draw two more wings off the center wing.

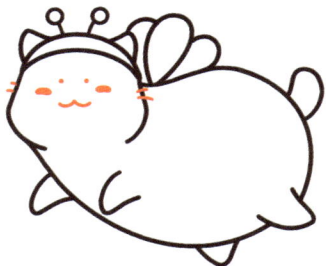

12. Give your kitty a fun facial expression.

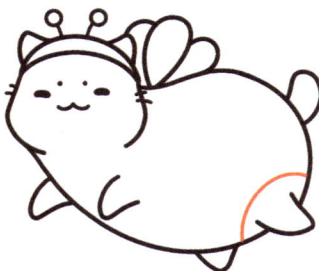

13. Draw a curved line around the outer-back leg to define the edge of the costume.

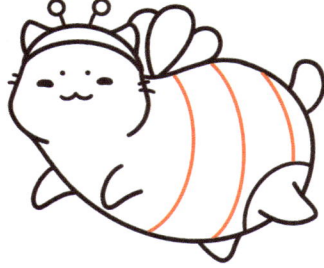

14. Add three slightly curved lines around the body for the stripes.

THE HONEY CAT

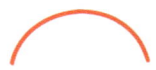

1. Start by drawing the top of the hood.

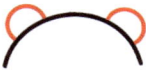

2. Add round ears to the hood.

3. Draw the sides of the hood.

4. Draw a curved line to define the shape of the hood and give it depth.

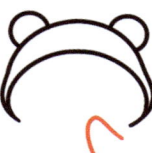

5. Draw a raised front leg on the right side, overlapping the face.

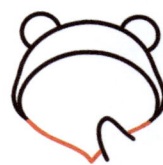

6. Draw two curved lines that converge at a point below the face for the top of the bear suit.

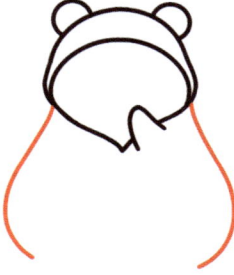

7. Draw the sides of the body.

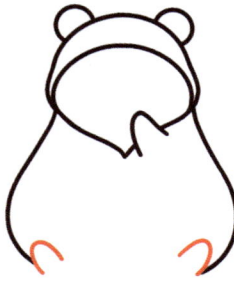

8. Add the back legs so that they're sticking up.

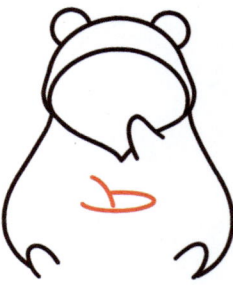

9. Draw an incomplete circle for the top of the honey pot and add a curved line going into it for the front leg.

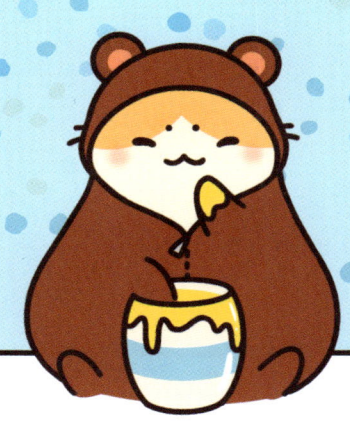

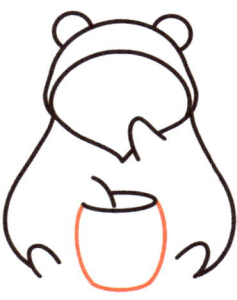

10. Complete the shape of the honey pot with three curved lines.

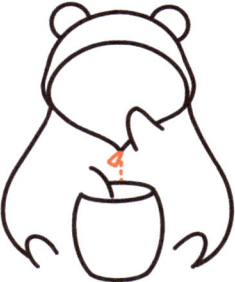

11. Add a zipper and pull details to the suit.

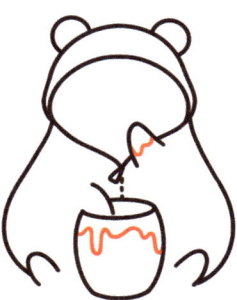

12. Draw the honey dripping around the top of the pot and on the raised leg.

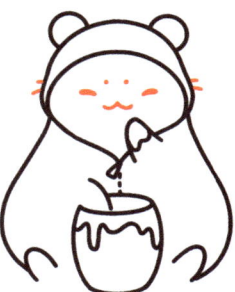

13. Finish by giving your kitty a fun facial expression.

THE UNIMEOW

1. Start by drawing the pointy horn that will sit on top of your kitty's head slightly tilted to the left.

2. Add curved lines to the horn to make it spiraled.

3. Draw the top of the head extending from each side of the horn, along with the ears.

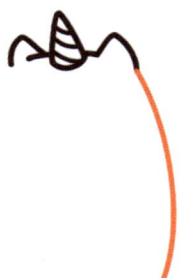

4. Draw the right side of the head and body.

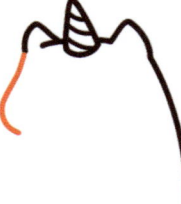

5. Draw the left side of the head.

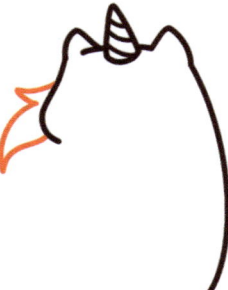

6. Draw the mane "behind" the left side of the head.

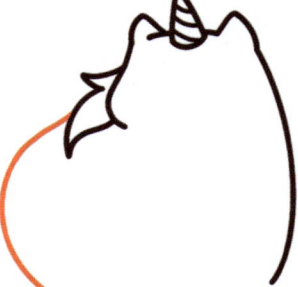

7. Draw the back of the body.

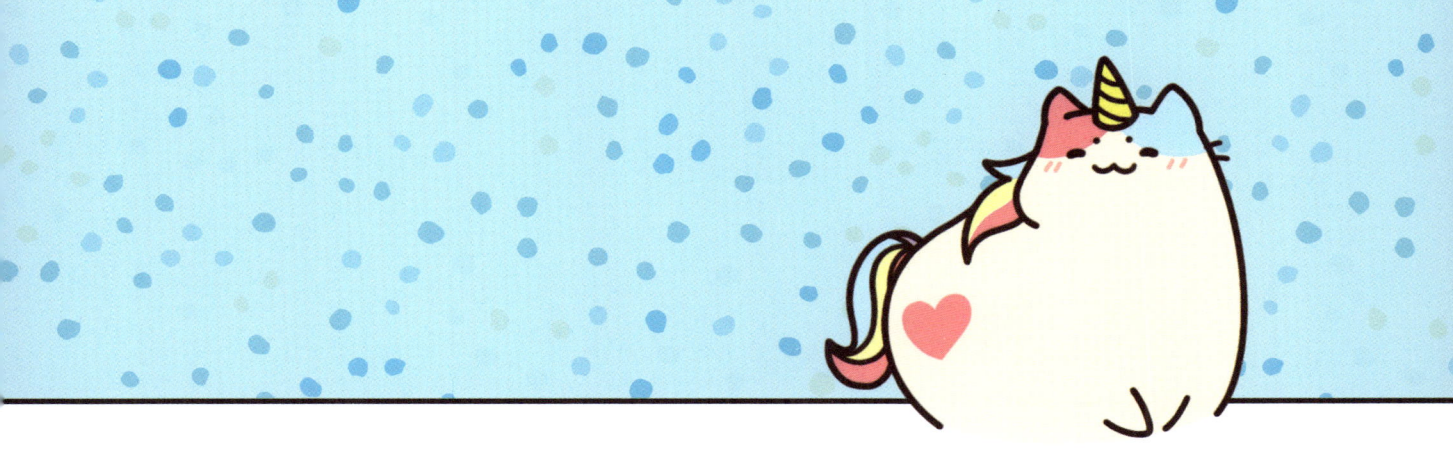

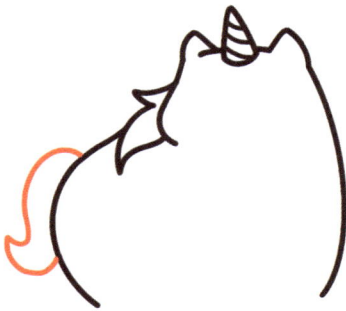

8. Add a long, thick tail.

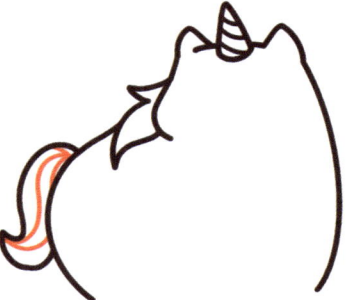

9. Give the tail texture with curved lines.

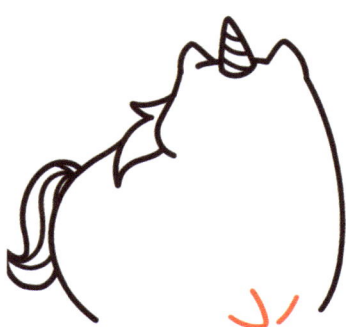

10. Draw the front legs.

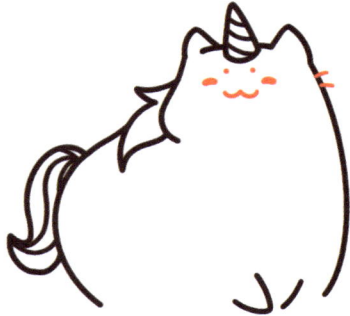

11. Finish by giving your kitty a fun facial expression.

THE ANGEL CAT

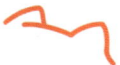

1. Draw the top of the head and the ears tilted to the right.

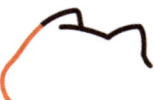

2. Draw the left side of the head.

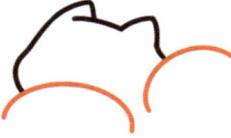

3. Draw two curved lines on the back of the kitty for the top of the wings.

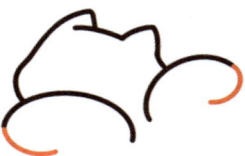

4. Continue drawing the shape of the wings by extending curved lines from the top lines.

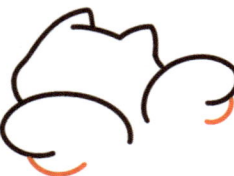

5. Draw two more curved lines to add to the shape of the wings.

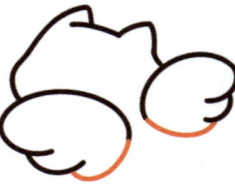

6. Complete the wings with two more curved lines.

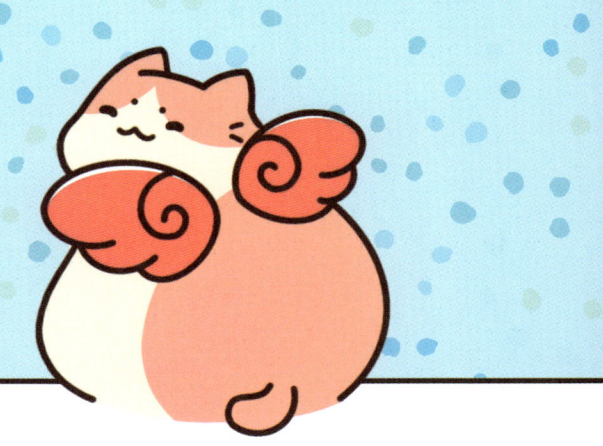

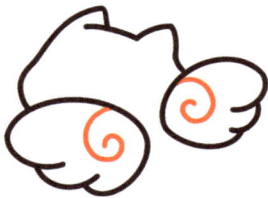

7. Draw spirals inside each wing for details.

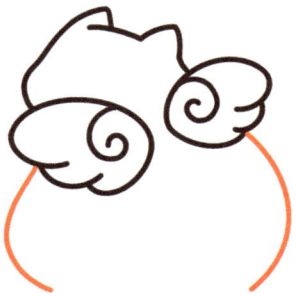

8. Draw the sides of your kitty's body.

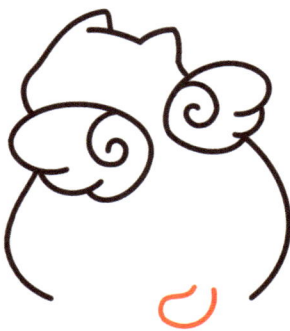

9. Add the tail.

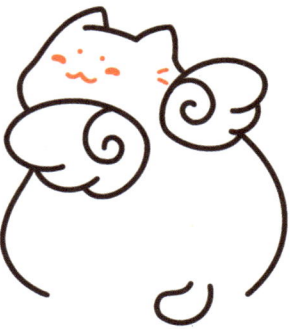

10. Finish by giving your kitty a fun facial expression.

THE ACCOUNTCAT

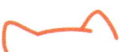

1. Draw the top of the head and the ears slightly tilted to the left.

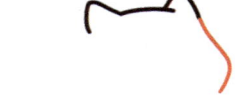

2. Draw the right side of the head.

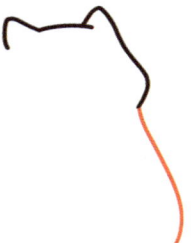

3. Draw the right side of the body.

4. Draw the left side of the head and body.

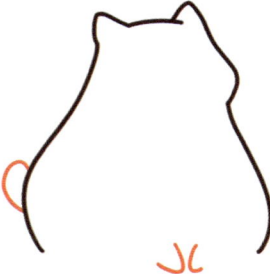

5. Position the front legs together in the center of the body. Add the tail.

6. Give your kitty a fun facial expression.

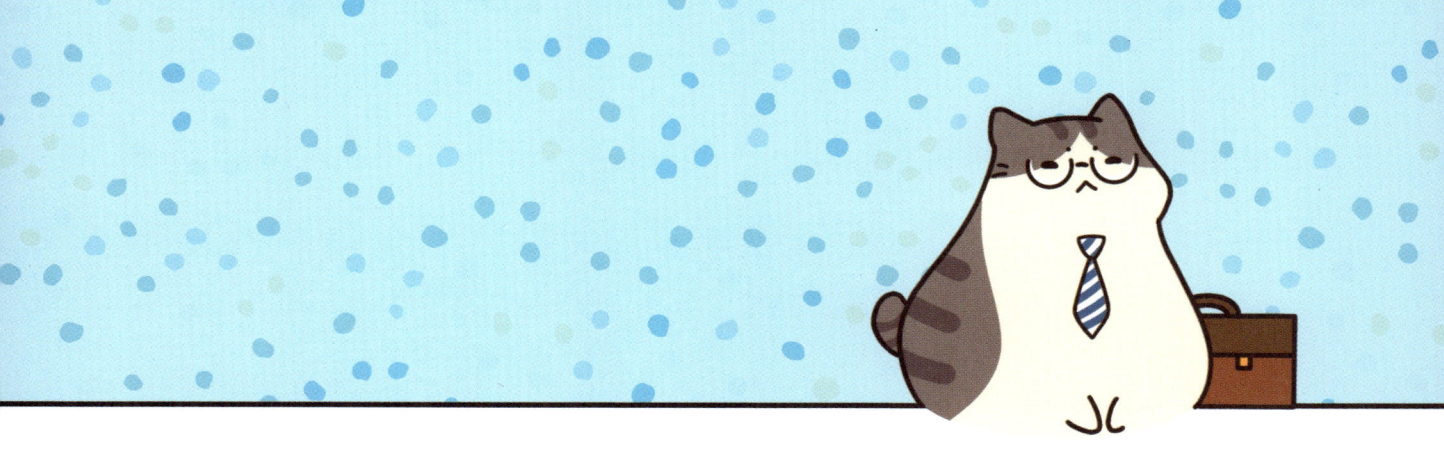

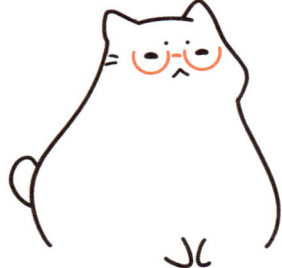

7. Add the glasses to the face as two semicircles below the eyes connected with a short line.

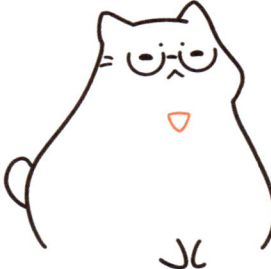

8. Draw a small triangle at the base of the neck for the knot of the tie.

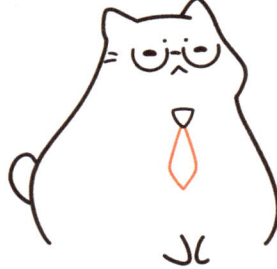

9. Draw an oblong diamond off the knot for the tie itself.

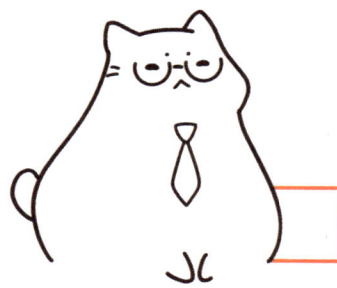

10. Start the briefcase off the right side of your kitty by drawing a three-sided square.

11. Add the handle as two curved, parallel lines.

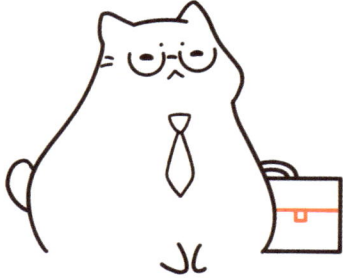

12. Finish by adding a horizontal line to the briefcase for the flap and a small three-sided square for the clasp.

THE HOLIDAY KITTY

1. Start by drawing the white fur on the front of the Santa hat as a narrow oval with slightly jagged edges.

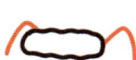

2. Add the ears to the sides and "behind" the fur.

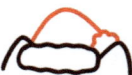

3. Complete the hat by drawing a mound shape between the ears that ends in a pom-pom on the right side.

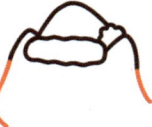

4. Draw the sides of your kitty's head.

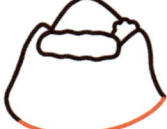

5. Connect the sides with a curved line for the edge of the top of the scarf that will wrap around your kitty's neck.

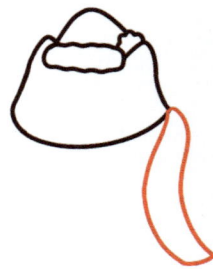

6. Draw the tail of the scarf off the right side of the head as two curved, parallel lines that are connected on the top and bottom.

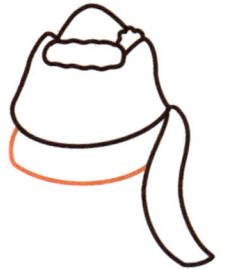

7. Complete the scarf by "wrapping" it around the neck with two curved lines.

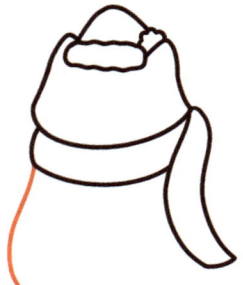

8. Draw the left side of the body.

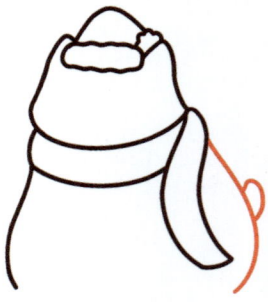

9. Draw the back of the body. Add the tail.

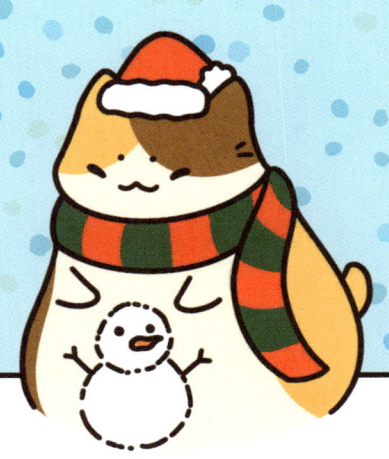

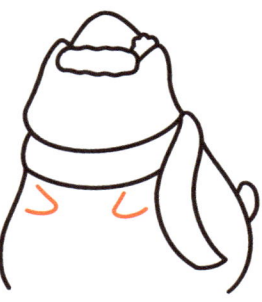

10. Draw the front legs, facing each other, below the scarf.

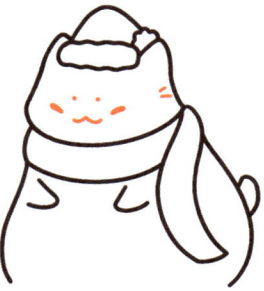

11. Give your kitty a fun facial expression.

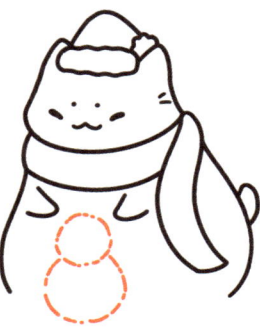

12. Draw a snowman shape on your kitty's belly.

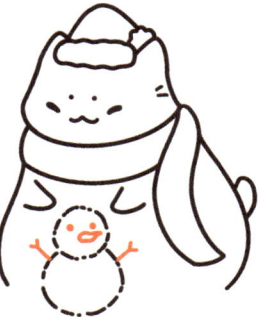

13. Finish by giving the snowman a face and arms.

THE SQUITTY

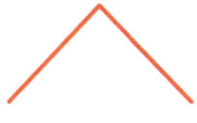

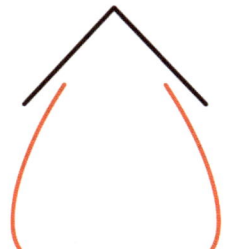

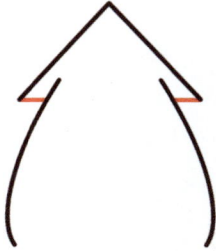

1. Start with the top of the squid's body by drawing an incomplete triangle.

2. Draw two convex lines for the sides of the squid's body, starting them inside the triangle.

3. Connect the top to the sides with short lines.

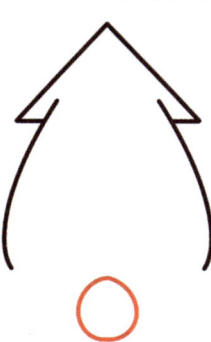

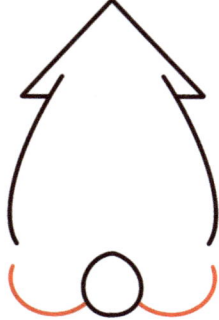

4. Center an oval below the body for the first leg.

5. Draw a curved line off each side of the oval for more legs.

6. Top those two curves with wavy lines.

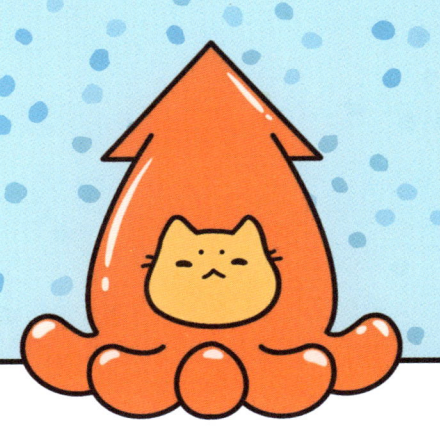

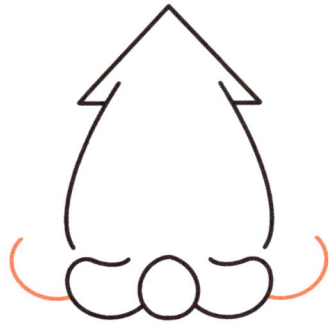

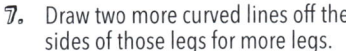

7. Draw two more curved lines off the sides of those legs for more legs.

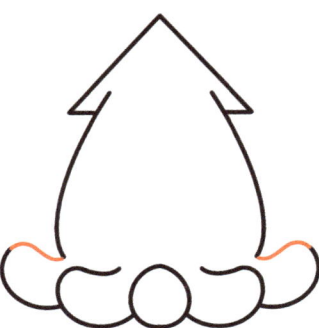

8. Top those curves with wavy lines too.

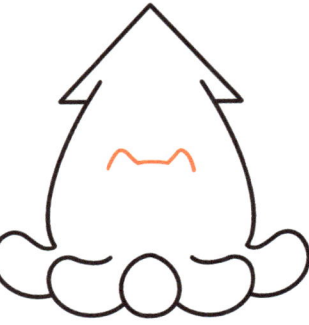

9. Draw the top of the head and the ears of your kitty in the center of the squid shape.

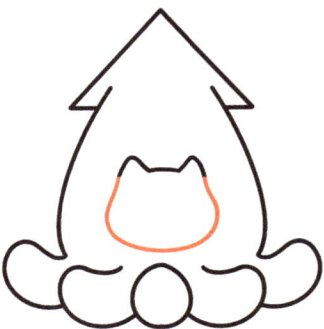

10. Complete the head of your kitty.

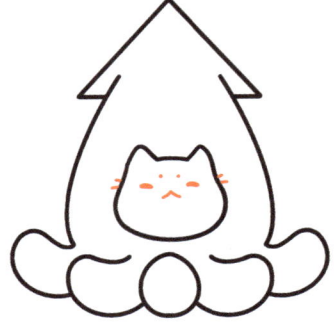

11. Finish by giving your kitty a fun facial expression.

THE LUCKY CAT

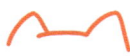

1. Draw the top of the head and the ears.

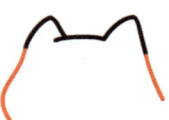

2. Draw the sides of the head.

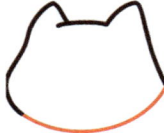

3. Connect the sides with a curved line for the top of the collar.

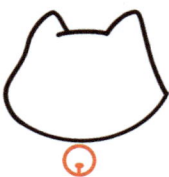

4. Draw the bell for the collar as a circle with a tiny T shape inside of it.

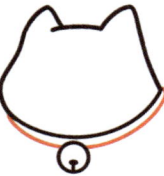

5. Draw the base of the collar as another curved line.

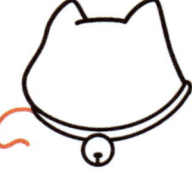

6. Draw the front leg on the left side raised up below the collar.

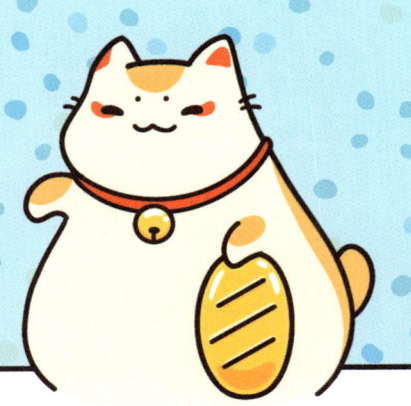

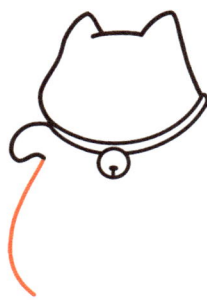

7. Draw the left side of the body.

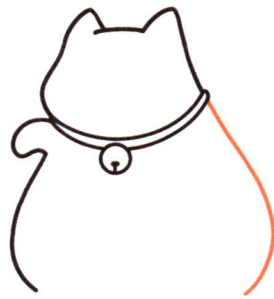

8. Draw the back of the body.

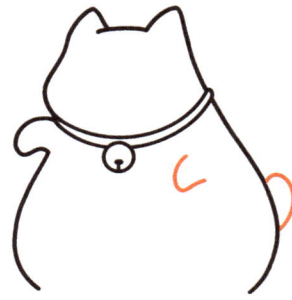

9. Add the other front leg, along with the tail.

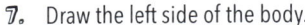

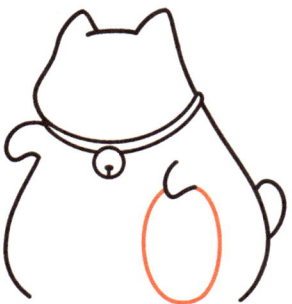

10. Draw an elongated oval off this leg for the koban (a Japanese gold coin).

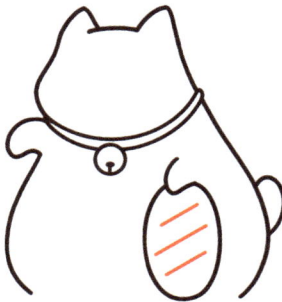

11. Add three diagonal lines to the coin for details.

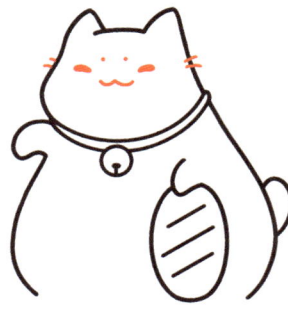

12. Finish by giving your kitty a fun facial expression.

THE MERMEOW

1. Draw the top of the head and the ears tilted to the left.

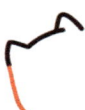

2. Draw the left side of the head.

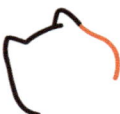

3. Draw the right side of the head.

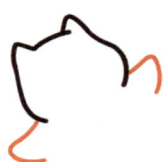

4. Draw the front legs held out to the sides.

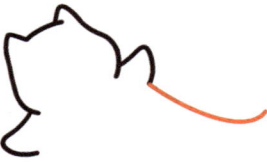

5. Draw the right side of the body with a curve at the end for the mermaid tail.

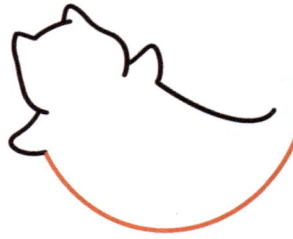

6. Draw the left side of the body, extending the curve for the tail.

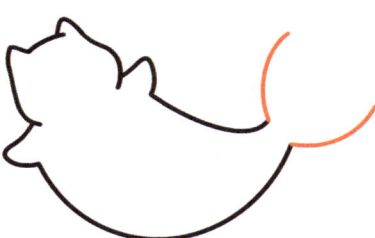

7. Add convex curves off the sides of the tail for the fin.

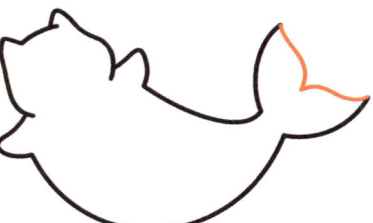

8. Complete the fin shape with more curved lines.

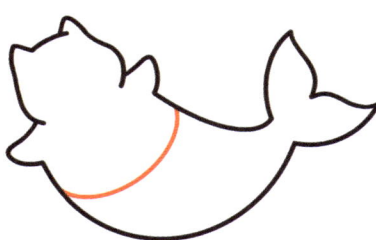

9. Draw a curved line across your kitty's body for the top of the tail.

10. Give the tail scales by drawing wavy lines.

11. Add short, slightly curved lines to the fin for detail.

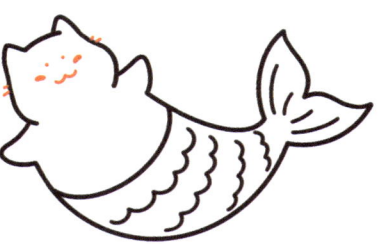

12. Finish by giving your kitty a fun facial expression.

THE DEVIL CAT

1. Start by drawing the pointy horns that will sit on the top of your kitty's head.

2. Close the bases of the horns with slightly curved lines.

3. Draw the top of your kitty's head between the horns, along with the ear on the left side.

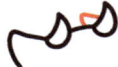

4. Draw an ear "behind" the horn on the right side.

5. Draw the sides of the head.

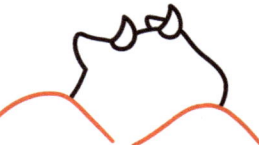

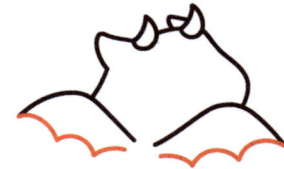

6. Draw two mound shapes on the back of your kitty for the top of the wings.

7. Add webbed lines to complete the bat-like wings.

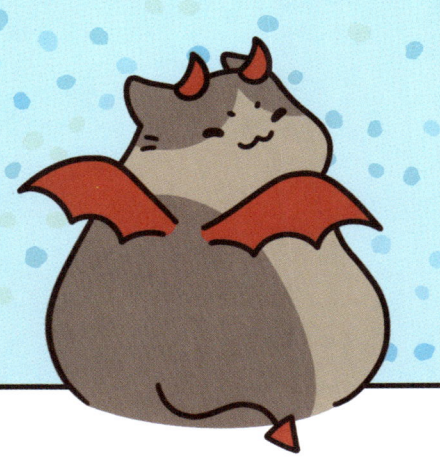

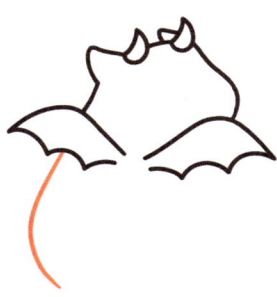

8. Draw the left side of the body.

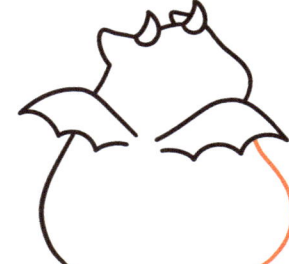

9. Draw the right side of the body.

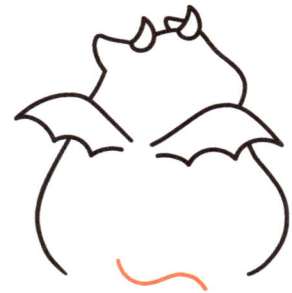

10. Add the tail as an S shape.

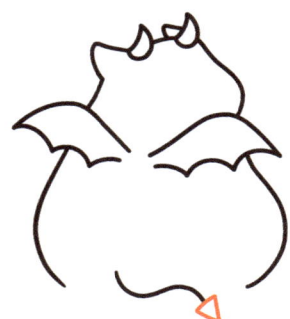

11. Draw a pointy triangle on the end of the tail.

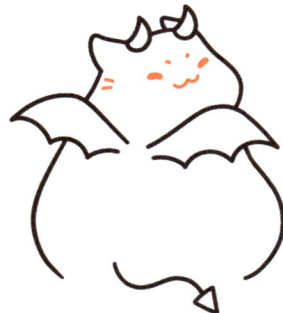

12. Finish by giving your kitty a fun facial expression.

THE CHEERKITTY

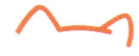

1. Draw the head and the ears slightly tilted to the right.

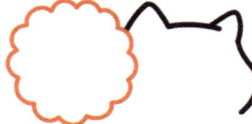

2. Draw the right side of the head.

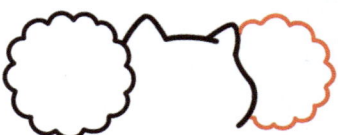

3. Draw the pom-pom as a circle with scalloped edges, overlapping the left side of the head.

4. Draw the second pom-pom "behind" the right side of the head.

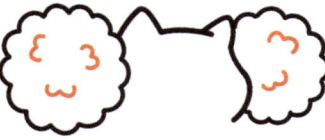

5. Add some E shapes to the pom-poms to give them texture.

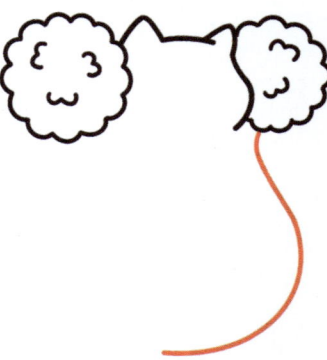

6. Draw the right side of your kitty's body.

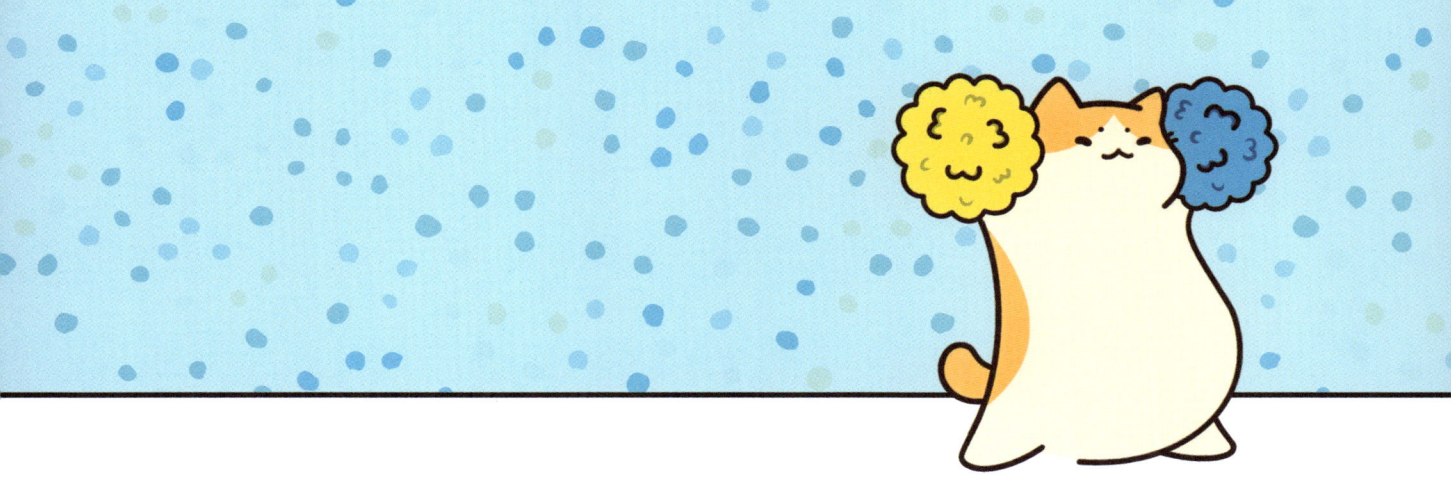

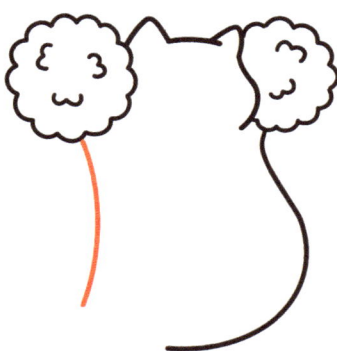

7. Draw the left side of the body as a slightly concave line.

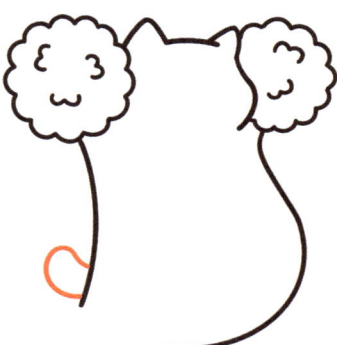

8. Add the tail.

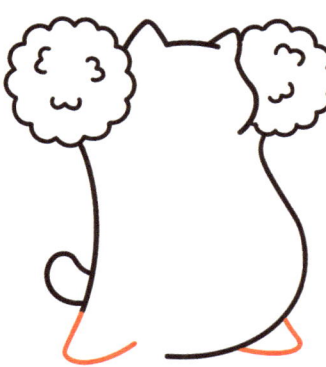

9. Draw the back paws splayed out.

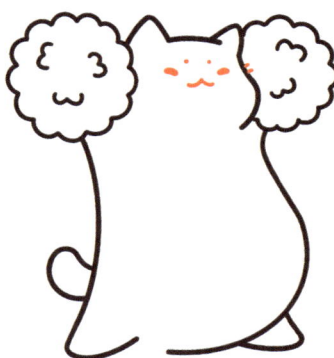

10. Finish by giving your kitty a fun facial expression.

SHARING THE LOVE

How do you spell "love"?

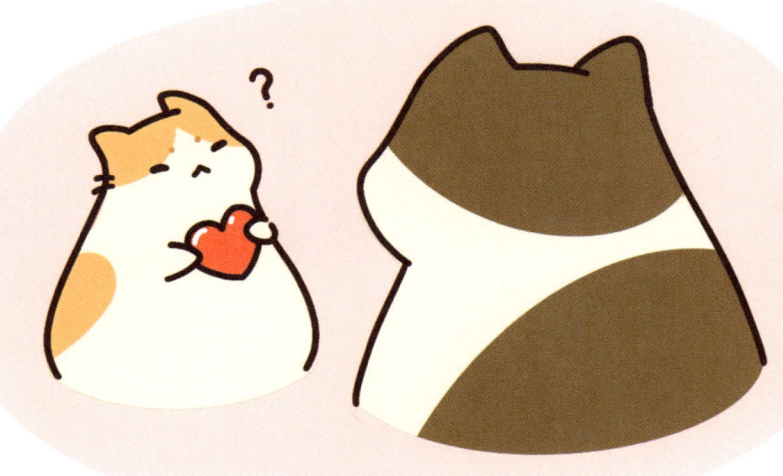

You don't spell it, you feel it.

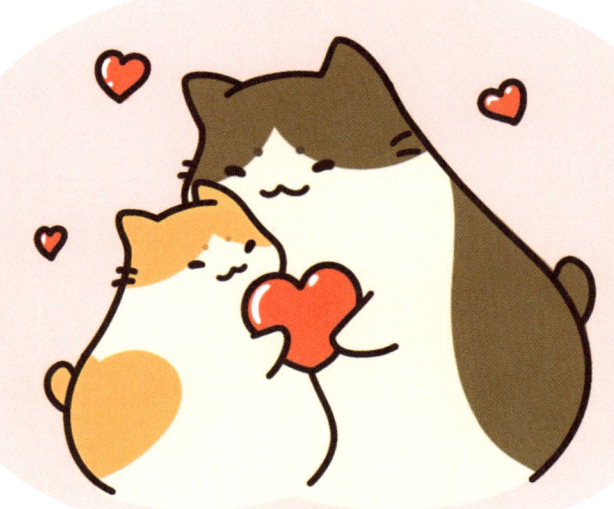

THE HUGGERS

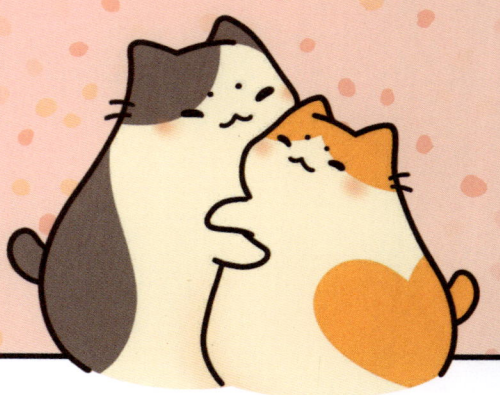

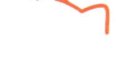

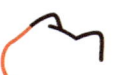

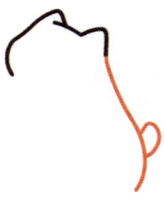

1. Starting with the kitty on the right, draw the top of the head and the ears slightly tilted to the right.

2. Draw the left side of the head.

3. Draw the back of the body. Add the tail.

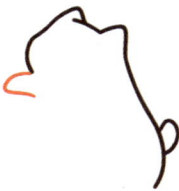

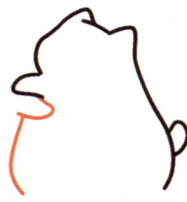

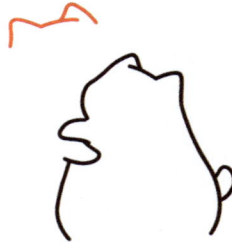

4. Draw the front leg so that it will be "hugging" the other kitty.

5. Insert the front leg of the kitty on the left directly below this leg for the embrace. Draw the front of the kitty on the right.

6. Draw the top of the head and the ears of the kitty on the left tilted to the left and above the kitty on the right.

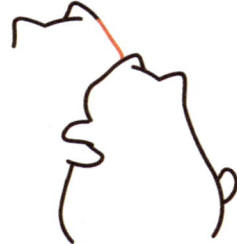

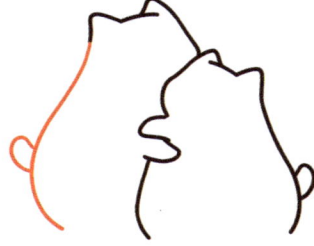

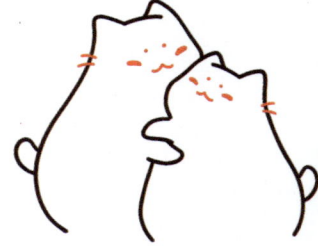

7. Draw the right side of this kitty's head.

8. Draw the back of this kitty. Add the tail.

9. Finish by giving your kitties fun facial expressions.

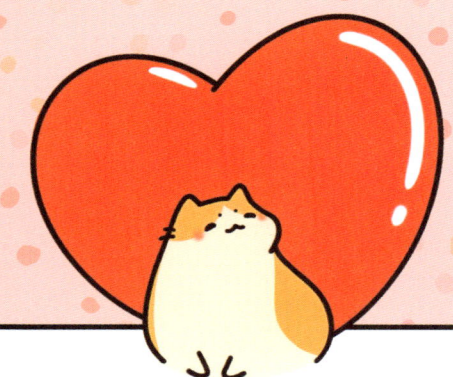

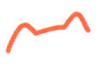

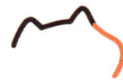

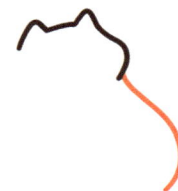

1. Draw the top of the head and the ears slightly tilted to the left.

2. Draw the right side of the head.

3. Draw the right side of the body.

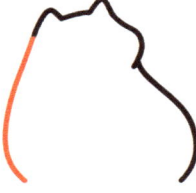

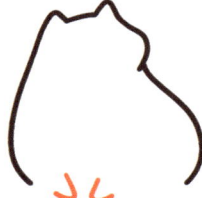

4. Draw the left side of the head and body.

5. Position the front legs together, closer to the left side of the body.

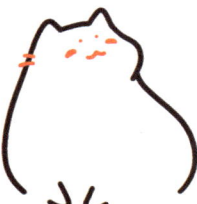

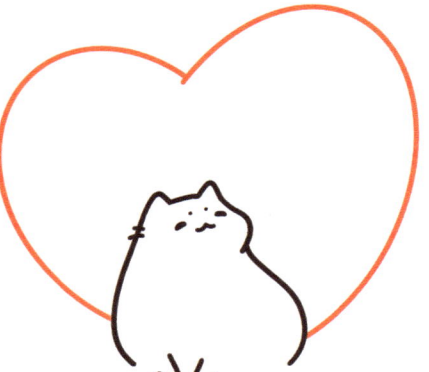

6. Give your kitty a fun facial expression.

7. Finish by drawing a large heart around your kitty.

THE SNUGGLERS

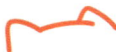

1. Starting with the kitty on top, draw the top of the head and the ears slightly tilted to the left.

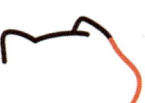

2. Draw the right side of the head.

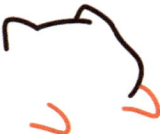

3. Draw the front legs so that they will be resting on the other kitty's body.

4. Draw the top of the head and the ears of the lower kitty.

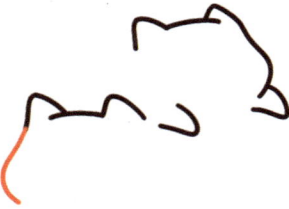

5. Draw the left side of this kitty's face.

6. Add curved lines angling in at each other for the tops of the front legs.

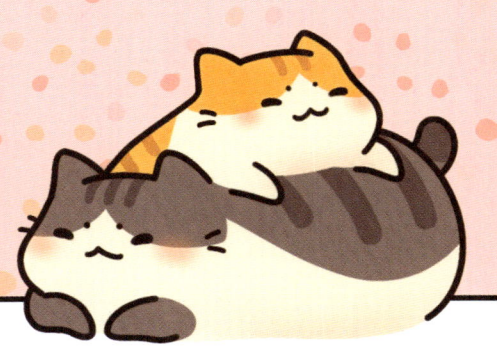

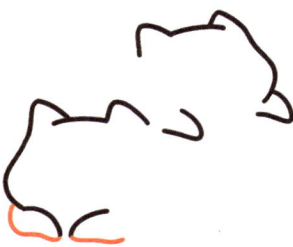

7. Complete the shape of the legs.

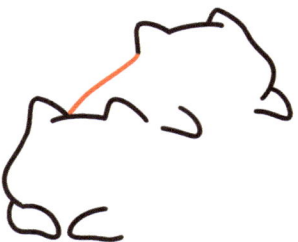

8. Draw a slightly curved line from the ear of the upper kitty to the top of the lower kitty's head.

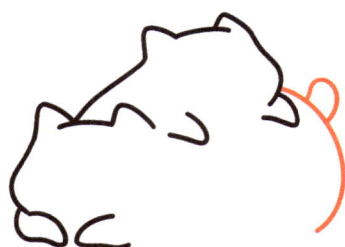

9. Draw the back of the lower kitty. Add the tail.

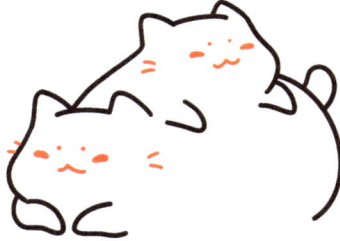

10. Finish by giving your kitties fun facial expressions.

THE PLAYMATES

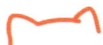

1. Starting with the upper kitty, draw the top of the head and the ears.

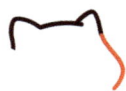

2. Draw the right side of the head.

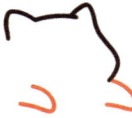

3. Draw the front legs so that they will rest on the brick wall.

4. Start drawing the brick wall with two connected straight lines.

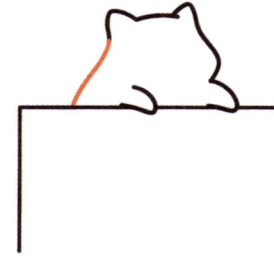

5. Draw the back of the upper kitty.

6. Draw the top of the head and the ears of the lower kitty, with the ears tilted back.

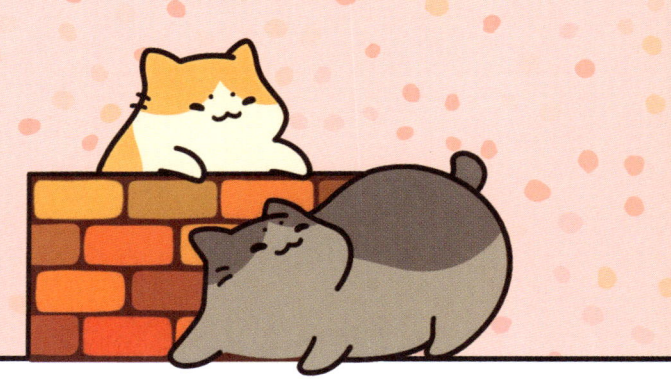

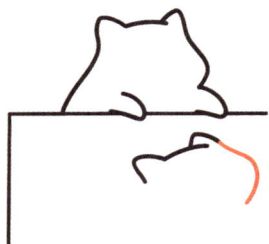

7. Draw the right side of this kitty's head.

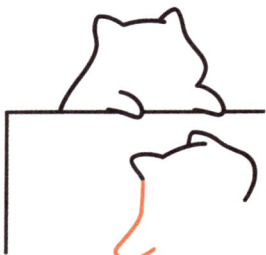

8. Draw the left side of the head, extending it into the front leg.

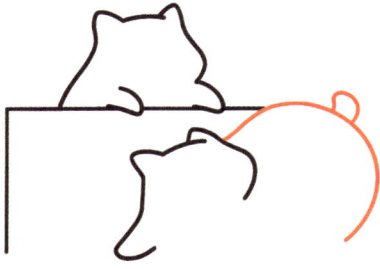

9. Draw the back of this kitty. Add the tail.

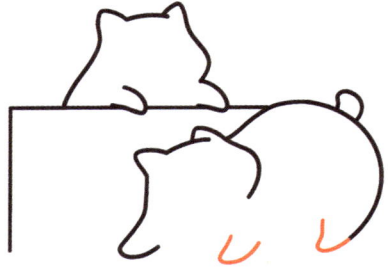

10. Add the outer-front and -back legs.

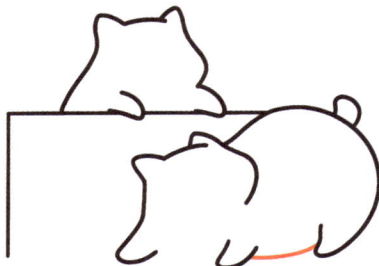

11. Draw the underside of the body.

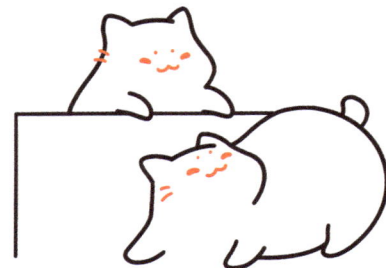

12. Finish by giving your kitties fun facial expressions.

THE ADMIRER

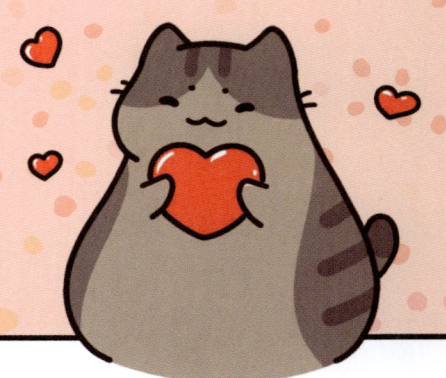

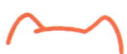

1. Draw the top of the head and the ears.

2. Draw the left side of the head.

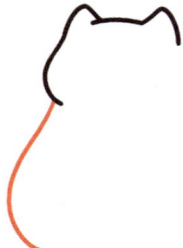

3. Draw the left side of the body.

4. Draw the right side of the head and body.

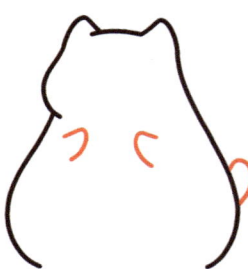

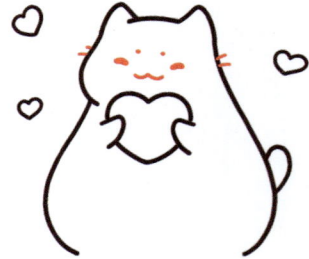

5. Add the front legs, facing each other, along with the tail.

6. Place a large heart between the front paws and add smaller hearts around your kitty.

7. Finish by giving your kitty a fun facial expression.

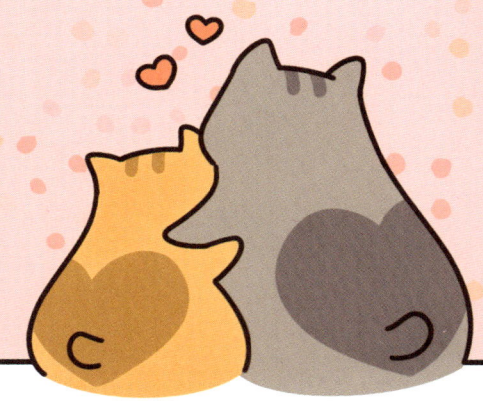

THE BESTIES

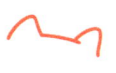

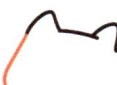

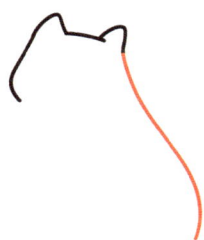

1. Starting with the kitty on the right, draw the top of the head and the ears tilted to the right.

2. Draw the left side of the head.

3. Draw the right side of the body.

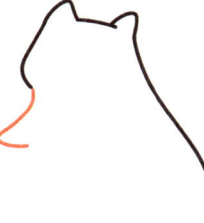

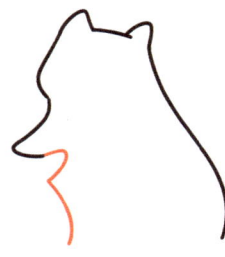

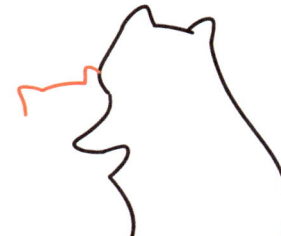

4. Draw the front leg "hugging" the other kitty.

5. Insert the front leg of the kitty on the left directly below this leg for the embrace. Draw the right side of the body of this kitty.

6. Draw the top of the head and the ears of this kitty slightly tilted to the left and below the other kitty.

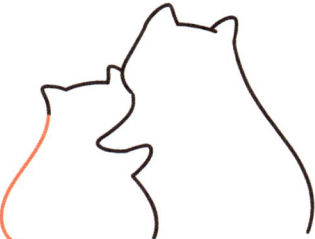

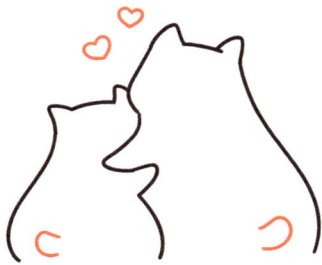

7. Draw the left side of this kitty's body.

8. Finish by adding the tails and a couple of hearts above the pair.

THE FAMILY

1. Starting with the kitty on the left, draw the top of the head and the ears slightly tilted to the left and back.

2. Draw the right side of the head.

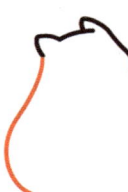

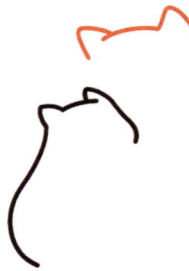

3. Draw the back of the body.

4. Draw the top of the head and the ears of the kitty on the right slightly tilted to the left and above the other kitty.

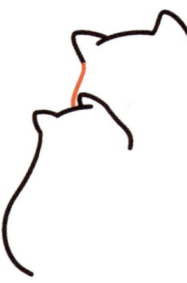

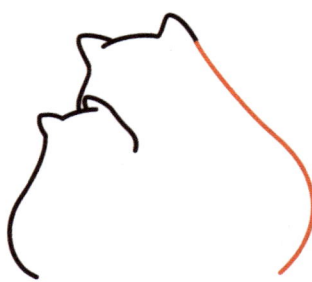

5. Draw the left side of this kitty's face.

6. Draw the back of this kitty's body.

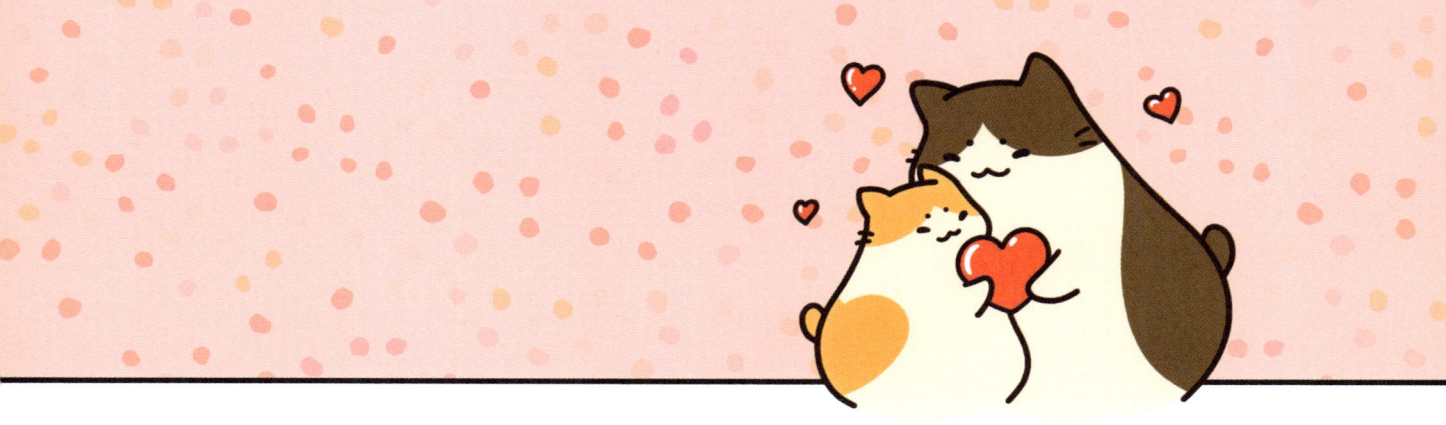

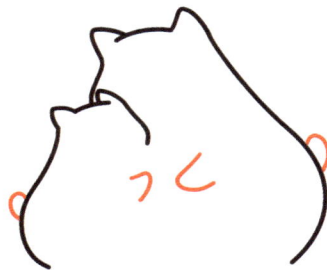

7. Add a front leg for each of the kitties, facing each other, along with their tails.

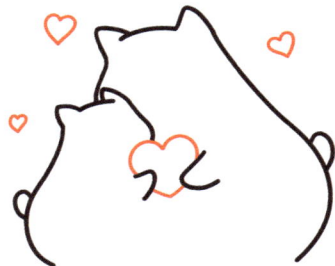

8. Place a large heart between their legs and draw smaller hearts around them.

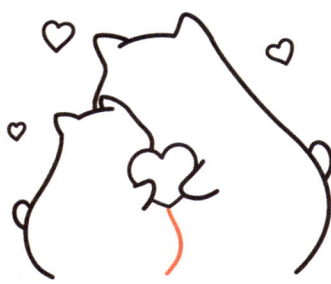

9. Draw the front of the kitty on the left.

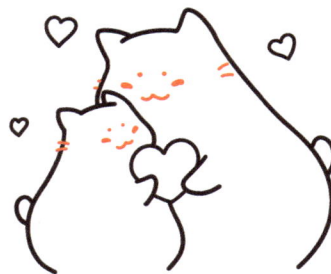

10. Finish by giving your kitties fun facial expressions.

DISCOVERING BREEDS

Where are your clothes?

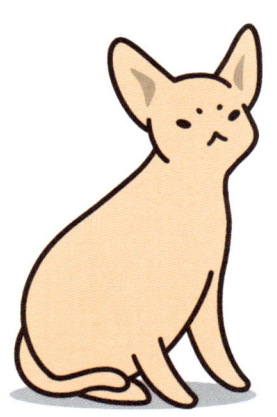

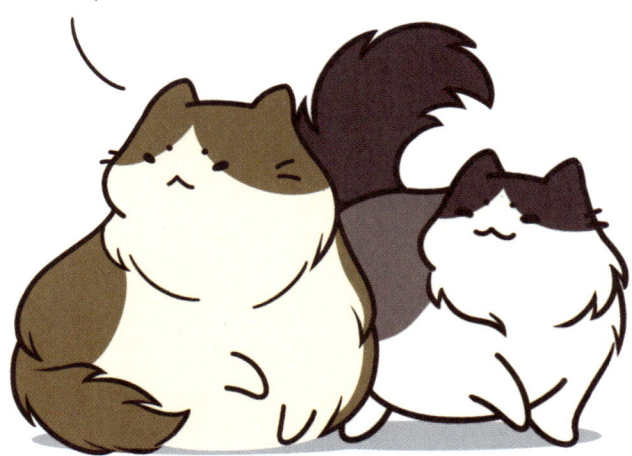

THE SIAMESE

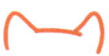

1. Draw the top of the head and the ears, making the ears extra upright.

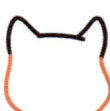

2. Draw the sides of the head.

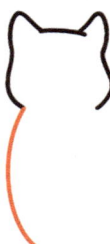

3. Draw the front of the body.

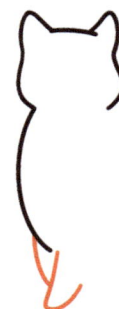

4. Draw the front legs so that the one on the right side overlaps the other one.

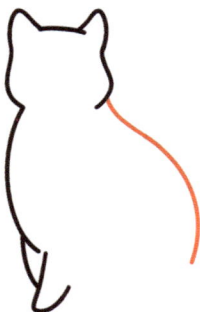

5. Draw the back of the body.

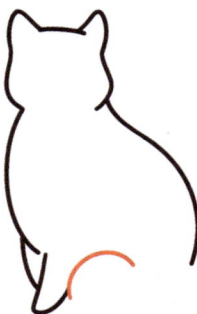

6. Start drawing the tail with a curved line for the curled end.

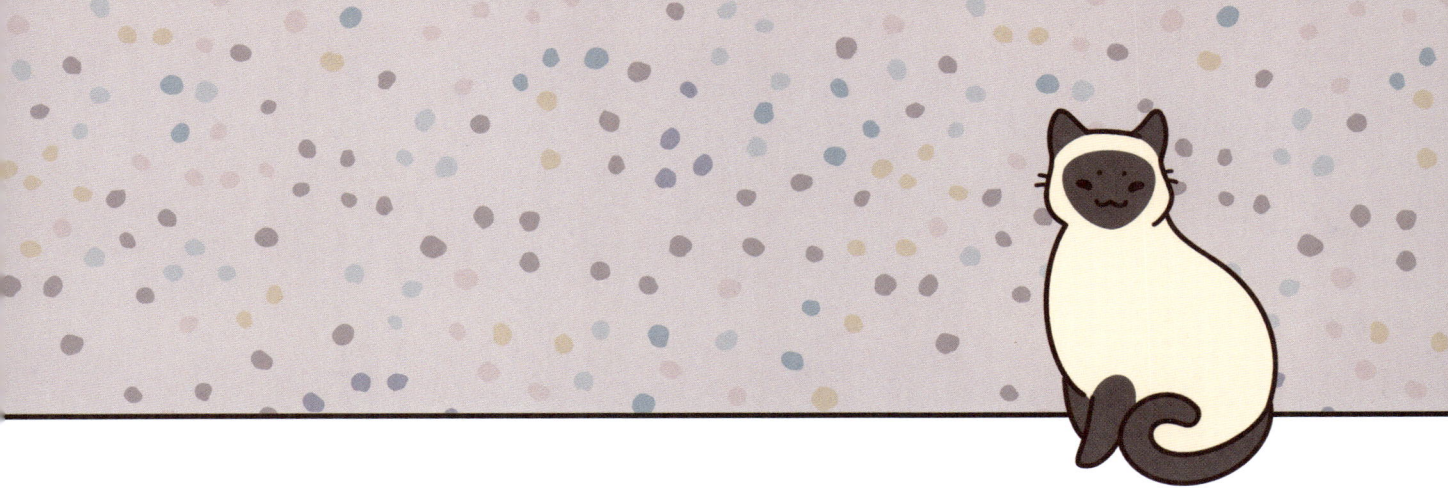

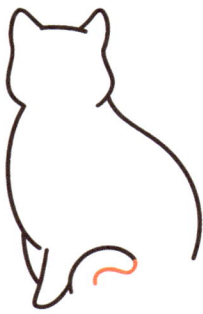

7. Continue drawing the curled end of the tail.

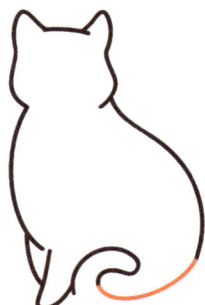

8. Connect the tail with the back of the body.

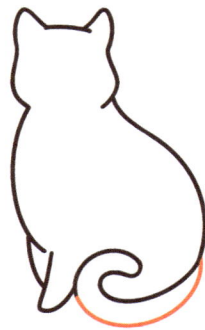

9. Complete the tail with the final curved line.

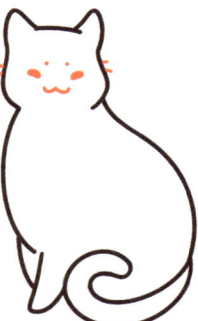

10. Finish by giving your kitty a fun facial expression.

THE SPHYNX

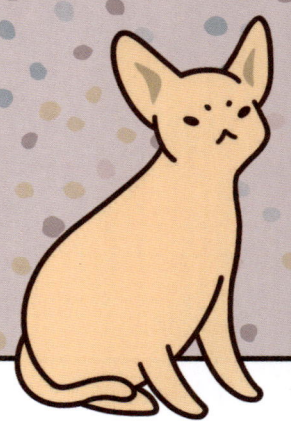

1. Draw the top of the head.

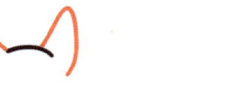

2. Draw the ears outsize.

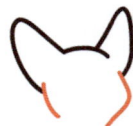

3. Draw the sides of the face, making the right side angular.

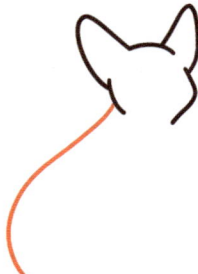

4. Draw the back of the body.

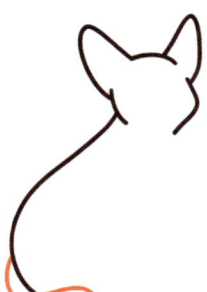

5. Add the long tail.

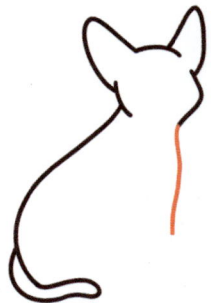

6. Draw the front of the body.

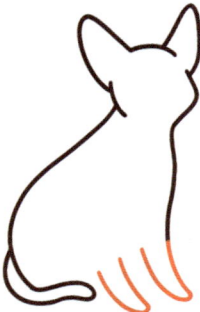

7. Draw the front legs.

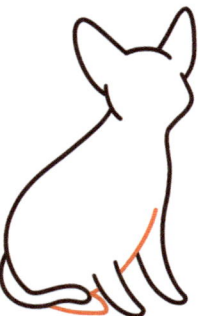

8. Draw the underside of the body. Add the outer-back leg.

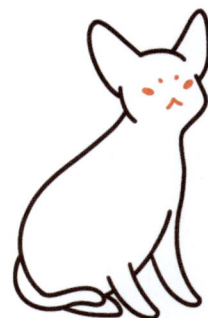

9. Finish by giving your kitty a fun facial expression.

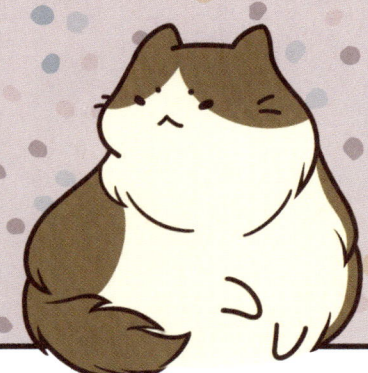

THE NORWEGIAN FOREST

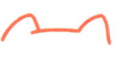

1. Draw the top of the head and the ears.

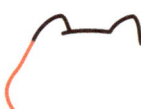

2. Draw the left side of the head.

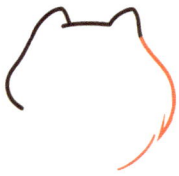

3. Draw the right side of the head, extending the line for the neck and adding some fur to it.

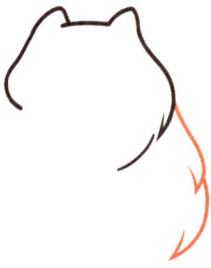

4. Draw the right side of the body and add some fur.

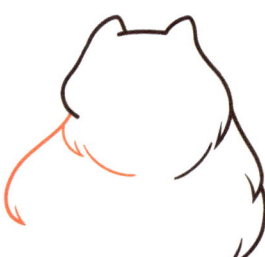

5. Draw the left side of the neck and upper body and add some fur.

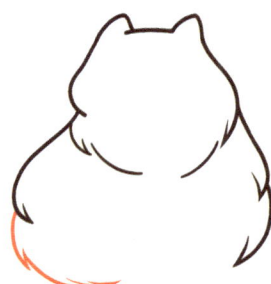

6. Draw the lower-left side of the body and add some fur.

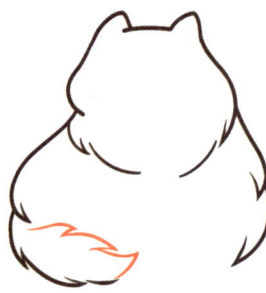

7. Add a bushy tail.

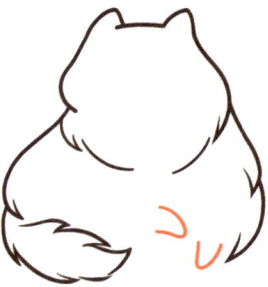

8. Draw the front legs slightly askew.

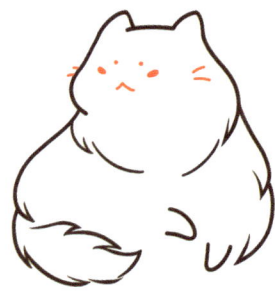

9. Finish by giving your kitty a fun facial expression.

THE EUROPEAN SHORTHAIR

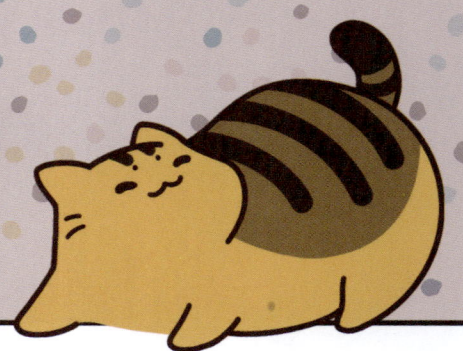

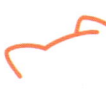

1. Draw the top of the head and the ears tilted to the left and back.

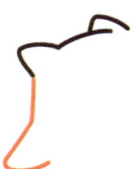

2. Draw the left side of the head, extending it into the front leg.

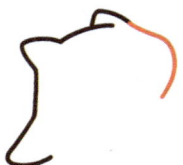

3. Draw the right side of the head.

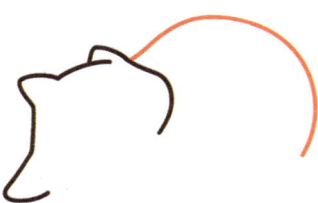

4. Draw the back of the body.

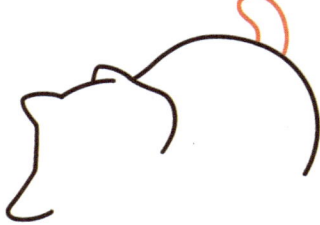

5. Add the tail.

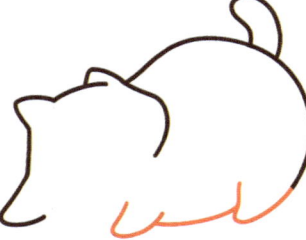

6. Draw the outer-front and -back legs, connecting them with the underside of the body.

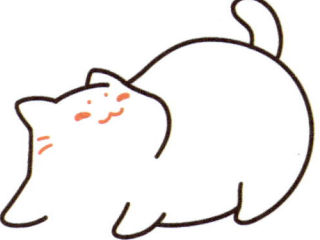

7. Finish by giving your kitty a fun facial expression.

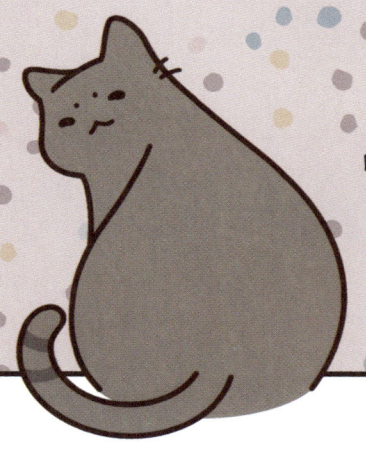

THE RUSSIAN BLUE

1. Draw the top of the head and the ears tilted to the left.

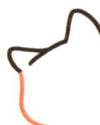

2. Draw the left side of the head.

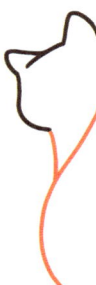

3. Draw the left side of the body, adding an inner curved line that defines the twisting of the body.

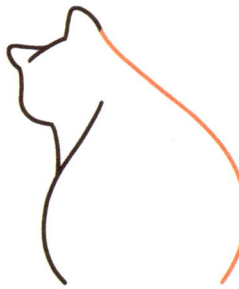

4. Draw the right side of the head and body.

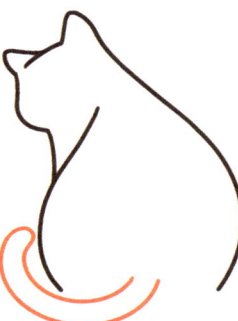

5. Add a long tail.

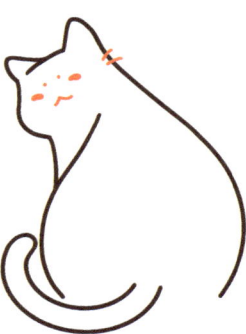

6. Finish by giving your kitty a fun facial expression.

THE AMERICAN SHORTHAIR

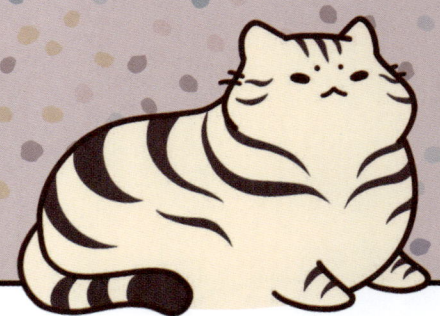

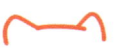

1. Draw the top of the head and the ears.

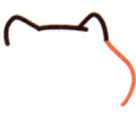

2. Draw the right side of the head.

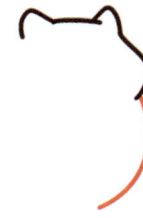

3. Draw the front of the body.

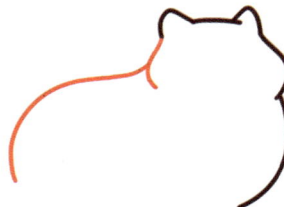

4. Draw the left side of the head and the back of the body.

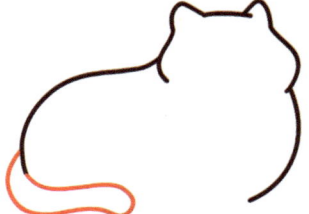

5. Add a long tail.

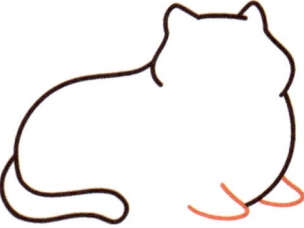

6. Draw the front legs.

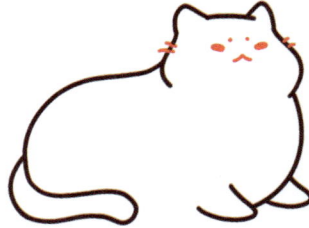

7. Finish by giving your kitty a fun facial expression.

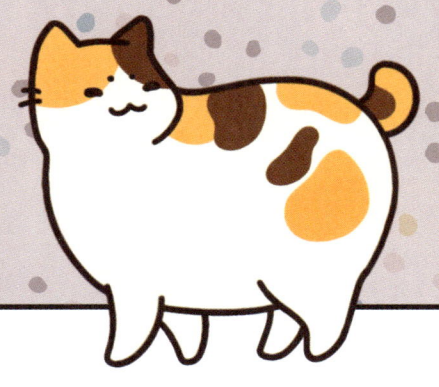

THE JAPANESE BOBTAIL

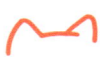

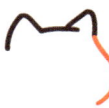

1. Draw the top of the head and the ears.

2. Draw the right side of the head.

3. Draw the back of the body. Add the tail.

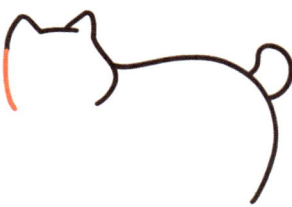

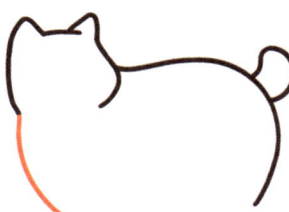

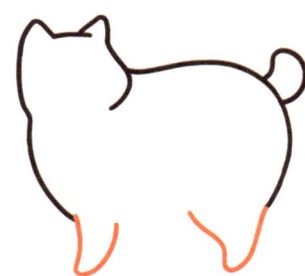

4. Draw the left side of the head.

5. Draw the front of the body.

6. Draw the outer legs.

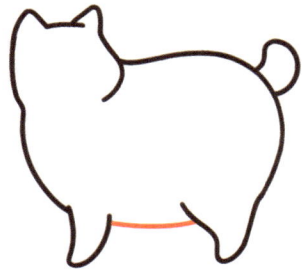

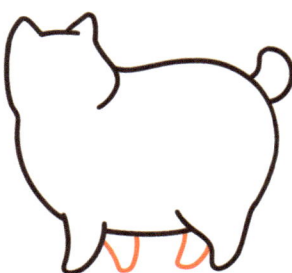

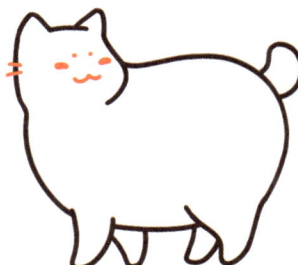

7. Draw the underside of the body.

8. Draw the inner legs.

9. Finish by giving your kitty a fun facial expression.

THE SNOWSHOE

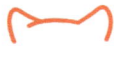

1. Draw the top of the head and the ears.

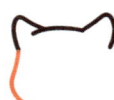

2. Draw the left side of the head.

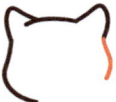

3. Draw the right side of the head.

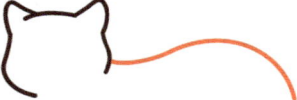

4. Draw the back of the body.

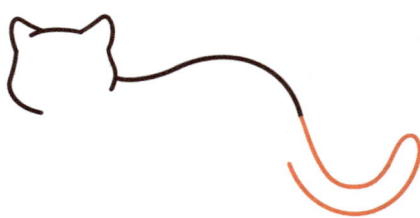

5. Add a long tail, extending it from the back of the body.

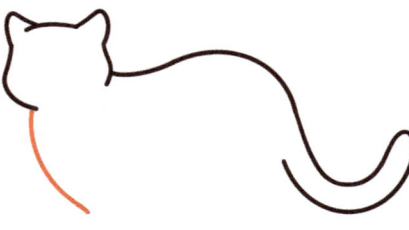

6. Draw the front of the body.

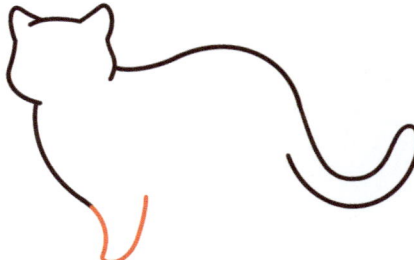

7. Draw the outer-front leg, extending it from the front of the body.

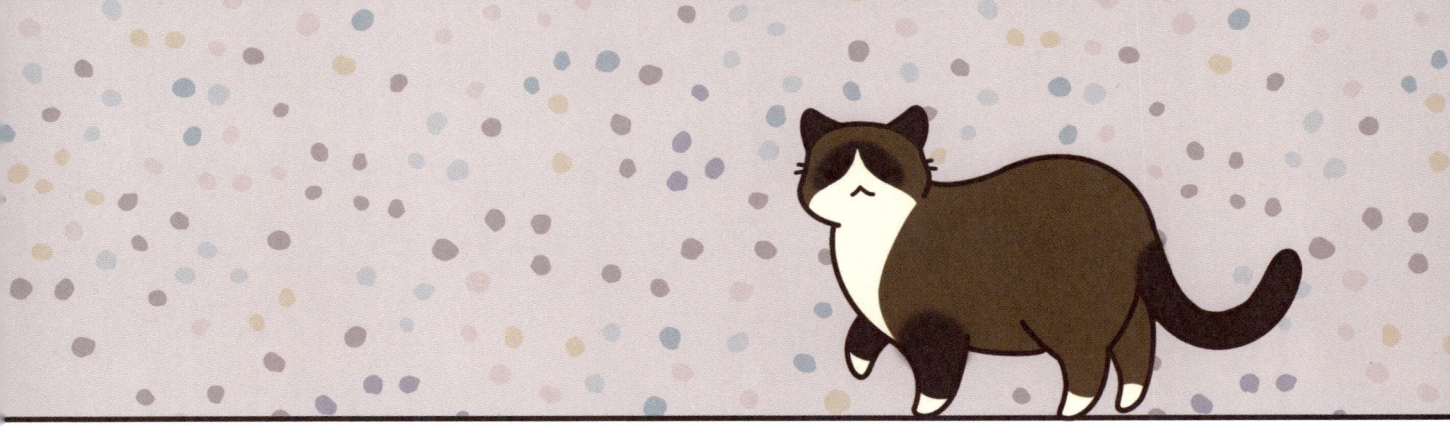

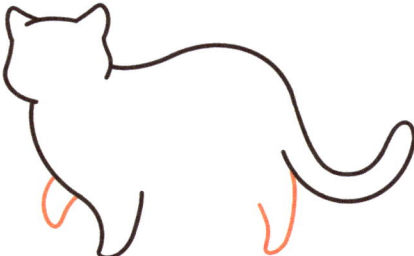

8. Draw the inner-front and outer-back legs.

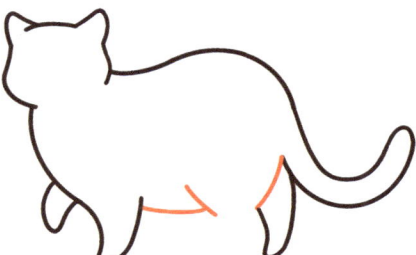

9. Draw the underside of the body and two curved lines defining the outer haunch.

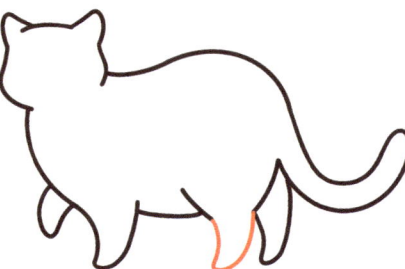

10. Draw the outer-back leg.

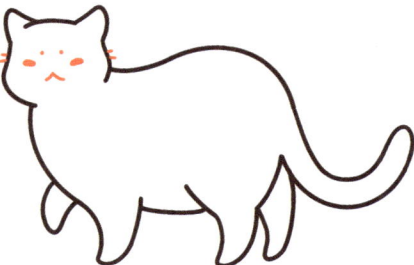

11. Finish by giving your kitty a fun facial expression.

THE RAGDOLL

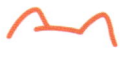

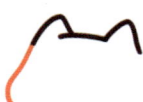

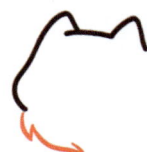

1. Draw the top of the head and the ears slightly tilted to the right.

2. Draw the left side of the head.

3. Extend a line from the head for the neck and add some fur.

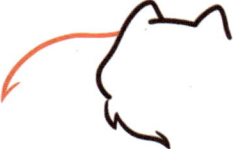

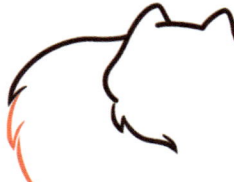

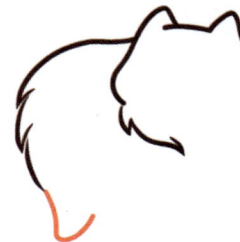

4. Draw the back of the body and add some fur.

5. Draw the haunch and add some fur.

6. Draw the back leg.

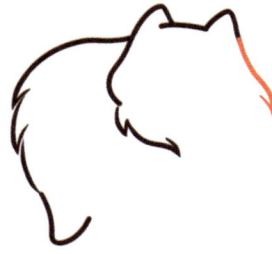

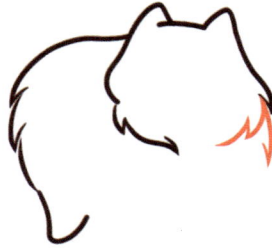

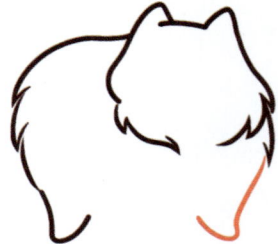

7. Draw the right side of the head and add some fur.

8. Draw the right side of the neck and the body and add some fur.

9. Extend the right side of the body into the leg.

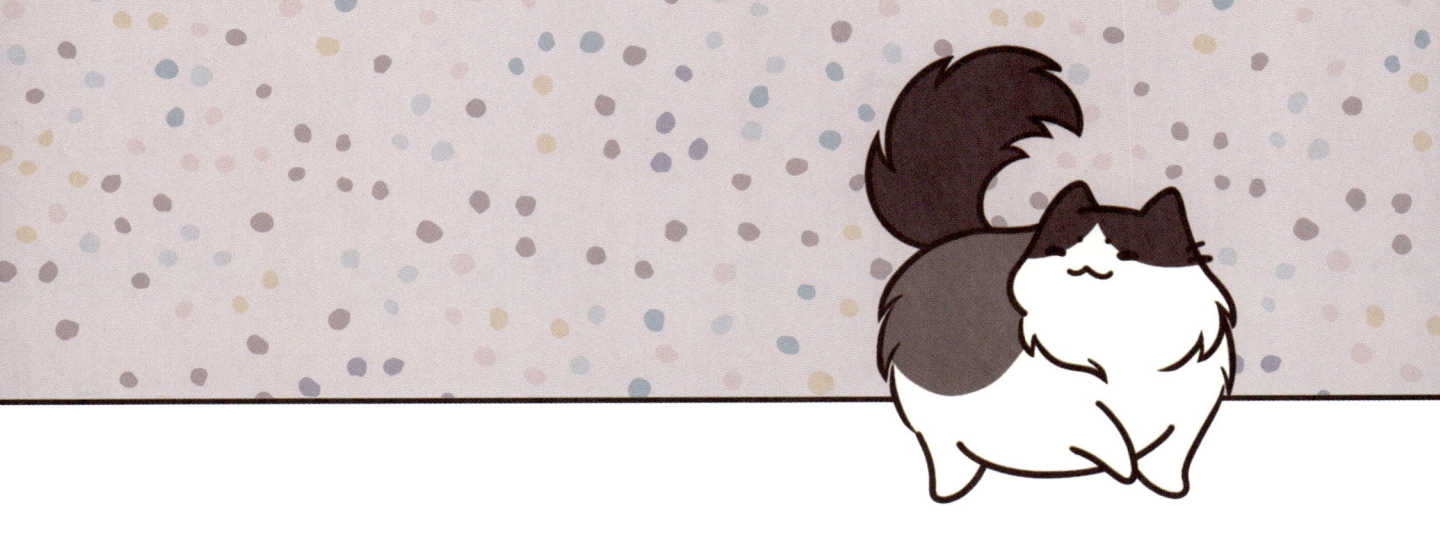

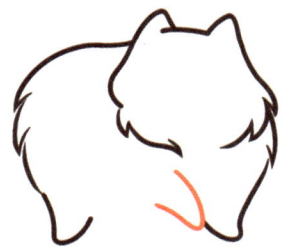

10. Draw the other front leg raised.

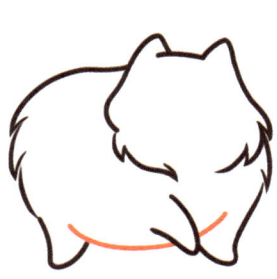

11. Draw the underside of the body.

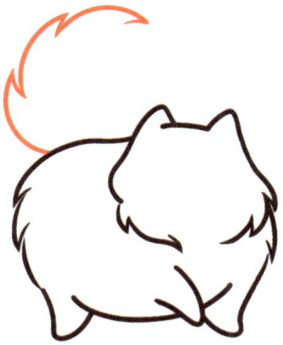

12. Start the tail with a line moving upward. Make it quite bushy.

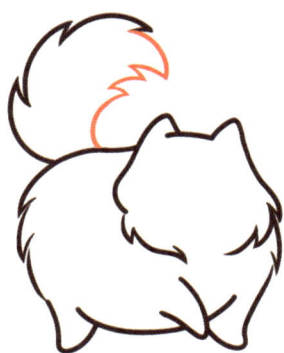

13. Add the other side of the bushy tail.

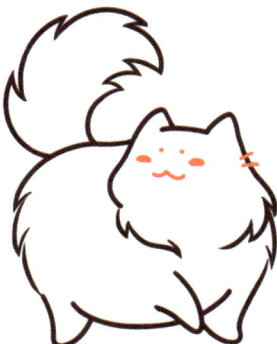

14. Finish by giving your cat a fun facial expression.

THE BENGAL

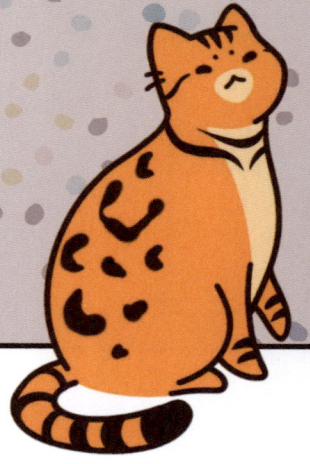

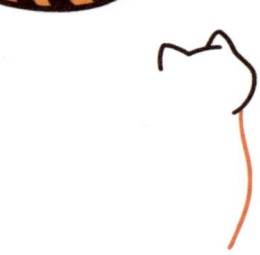

1. Draw the top of the head and the ears tilted to the left.

2. Draw the right side of the head.

3. Draw the front of the body.

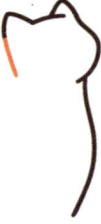

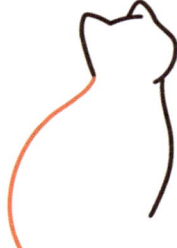

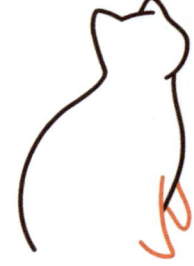

4. Draw the left side of the head.

5. Draw the back of the body.

6. Draw the front legs.

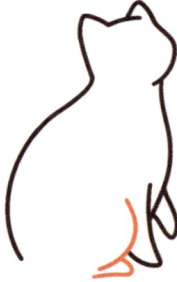

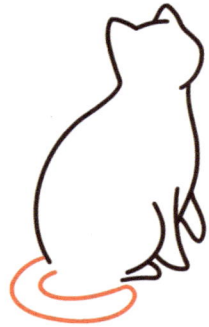

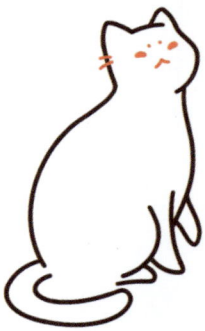

7. Draw a curved line to define the haunch. Add the outer-back leg.

8. Add a long tail.

9. Finish by giving your kitty a fun facial expression.

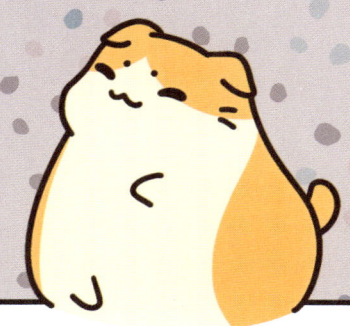

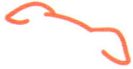

1. Draw the top of the head and the ears tilted to the right. The ears should be drawn flatter for the "fold" effect.

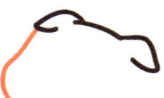

2. Draw the left side of the head.

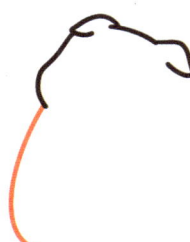

3. Draw the left side of the body.

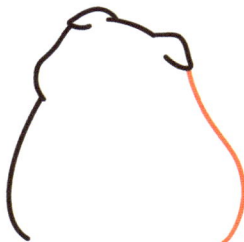

4. Draw the back of the body.

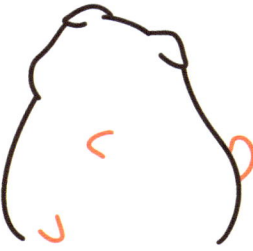

5. Add the tail and the front legs, with one placed higher than the other.

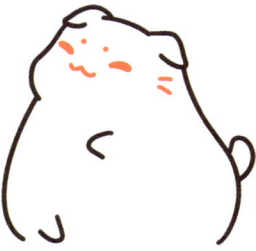

6. Finish by giving your kitty a fun facial expression.

BON APPÉTIT

The more you weigh,
the harder you are to kidnap.

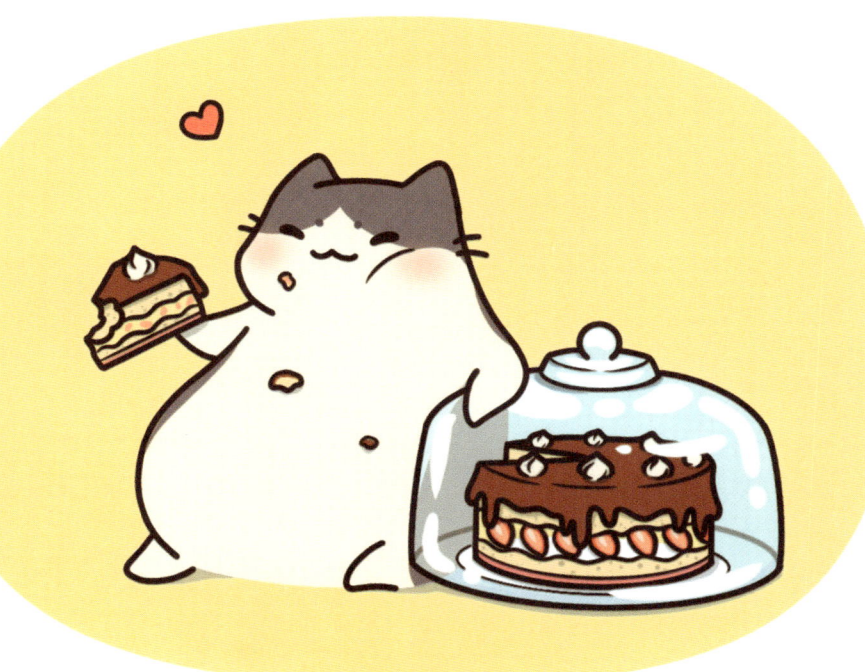

Stay safe. Eat cake.

KITTY CHEESEBURGER

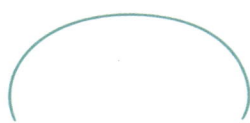

1. Draw a semioval for the outline of the top bun.

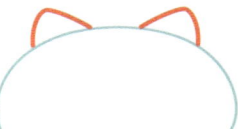

2. Add the ears.

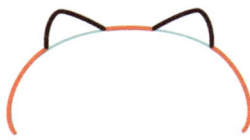

3. Draw the top and sides of the bun.

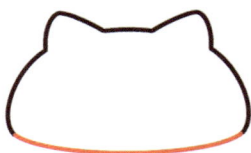

4. Connect the sides with a slightly curved line.

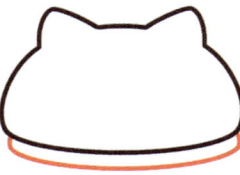

5. Draw another curved line below the bun for the tomato slice.

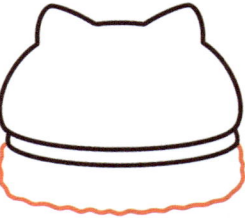

6. Add the hamburger patty, giving it slightly jagged edges.

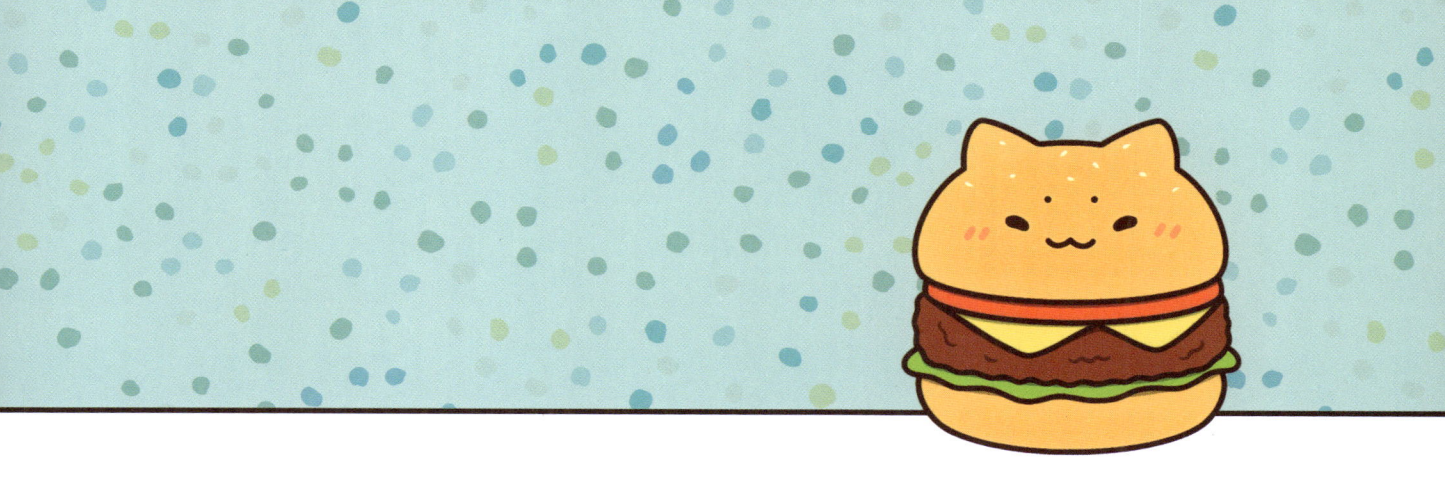

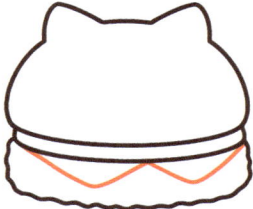

7. Draw two angular lines on the patty for the cheese slices.

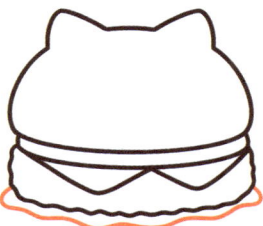

8. Draw a wavy line below the patty for the lettuce.

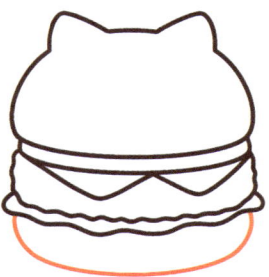

9. Add the bottom bun.

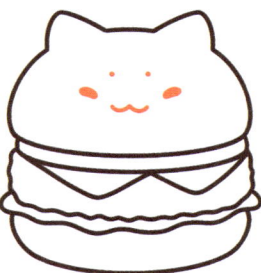

10. Finish by giving your cheeseburger a fun facial expression.

KITTY-SIDE UP

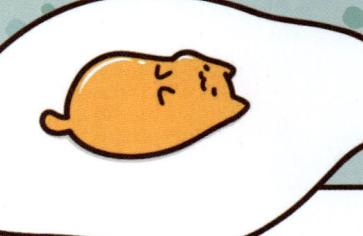

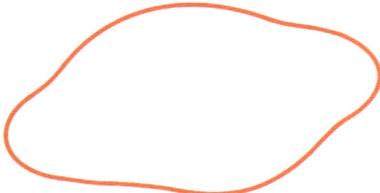

1. Draw the egg white as an amoeba-like shape.

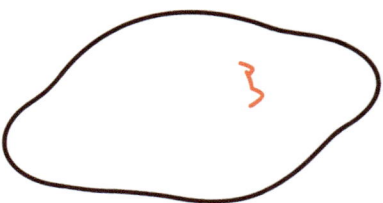

2. Draw the top of the head and the ears of the kitty yolk.

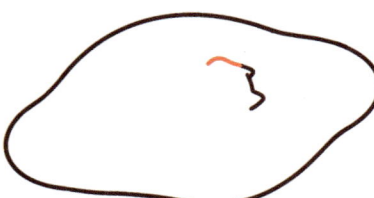

3. Draw the left side of the head.

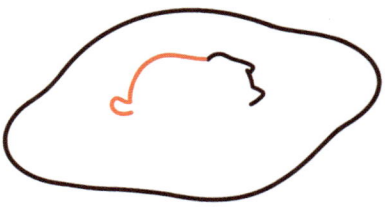

4. Draw the left side of the body with the tail.

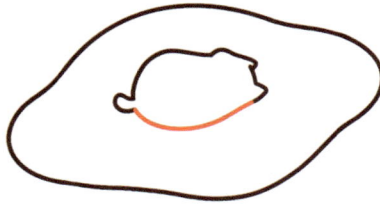

5. Draw the right side of the body.

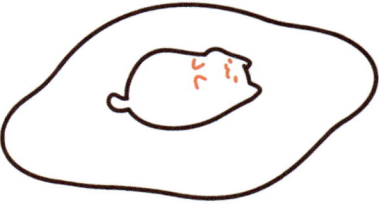

6. Finish by drawing the front legs, facing each other, and giving your fried egg a fun facial expression.

CORN CAT

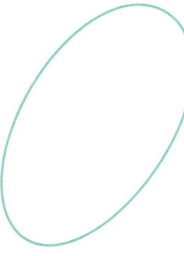

1. Draw a slanted oval for the outline of the corn dog.

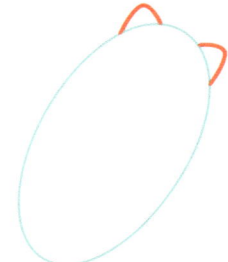

2. Add the ears.

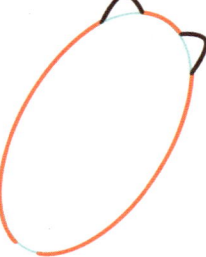

3. Draw the top and sides of the corn dog.

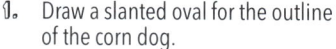

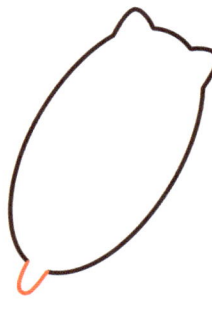

4. Add the "tail."

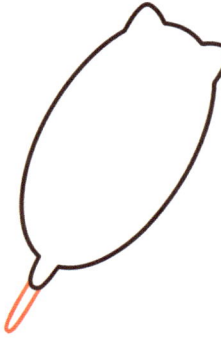

5. Draw the stick below the tail.

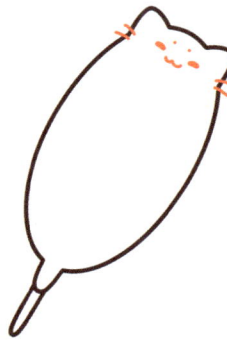

6. Finishing by giving your corn dog a fun facial expression.

KITTY MACARON

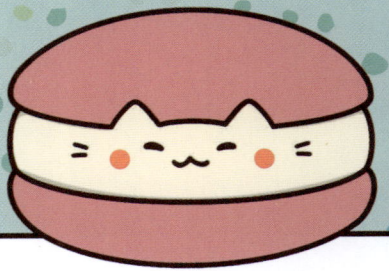

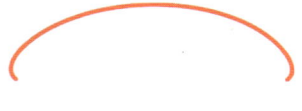

1. Draw a semioval for the top shell of the macaron.

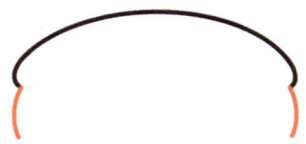

2. Add two curved lines for the filling.

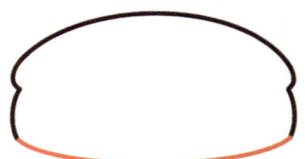

3. Connect the lines for the filling with a slightly curved line.

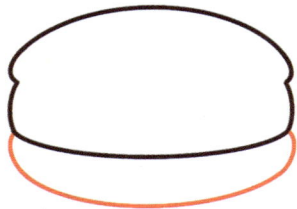

4. Draw the bottom shell of the macaron.

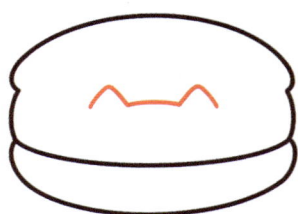

5. Draw the top of the head and the ears of the kitty between the filling and the top shell.

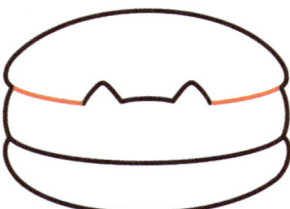

6. Extend lines from the sides of the ears to complete the shape of the top shell.

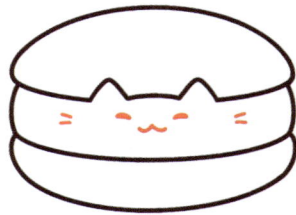

7. Finish by giving your macaron a fun facial expression.

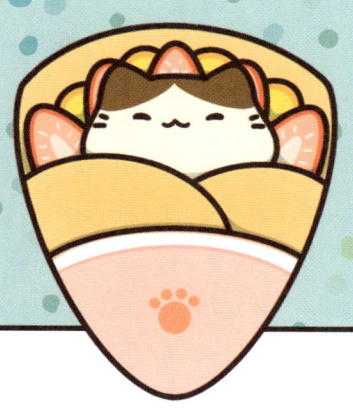

KITTY CREPE

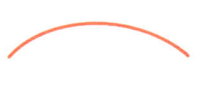

1. Draw the top of the crepe.

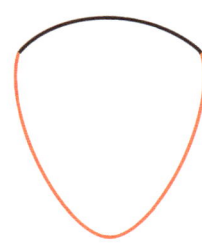

2. Draw a V shape for the rest of the crepe shape.

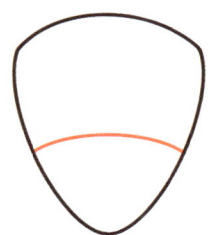

3. Draw a slightly curved line a little more than halfway down from the top for the wrapper.

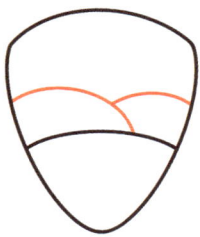

4. Draw two curved lines above the wrapper for the folds of the crepe.

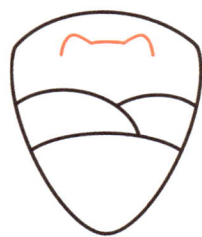

5. Draw the top of the head and the ears of the kitty.

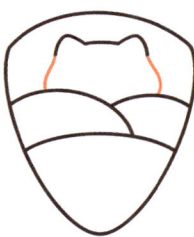

6. Draw the sides of the head.

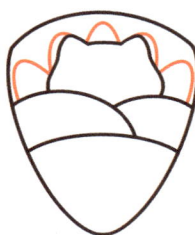

7. Add five rounded shapes "behind" the kitty's head for the strawberry slices.

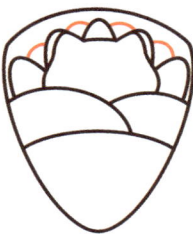

8. Add four more rounded shapes between the strawberry slices for the custard.

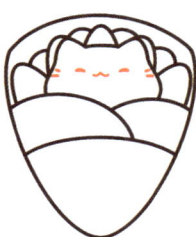

9. Finish by giving your crepe a fun facial expression.

CATUCCINO

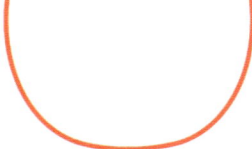

1. Draw the mug as a U shape.

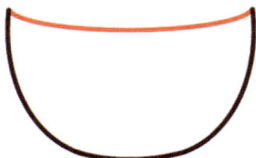

2. Draw a slightly curved line for the top of the mug.

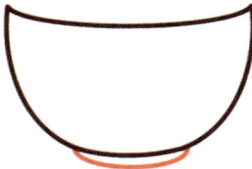

3. Draw a smaller curved line for the base of the mug.

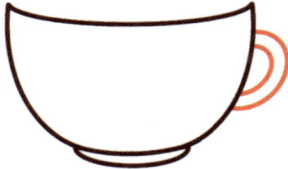

4. Add the handle to the right side of the mug as curved, parallel lines.

5. Draw the back of the kitty.

6. Add the tail.

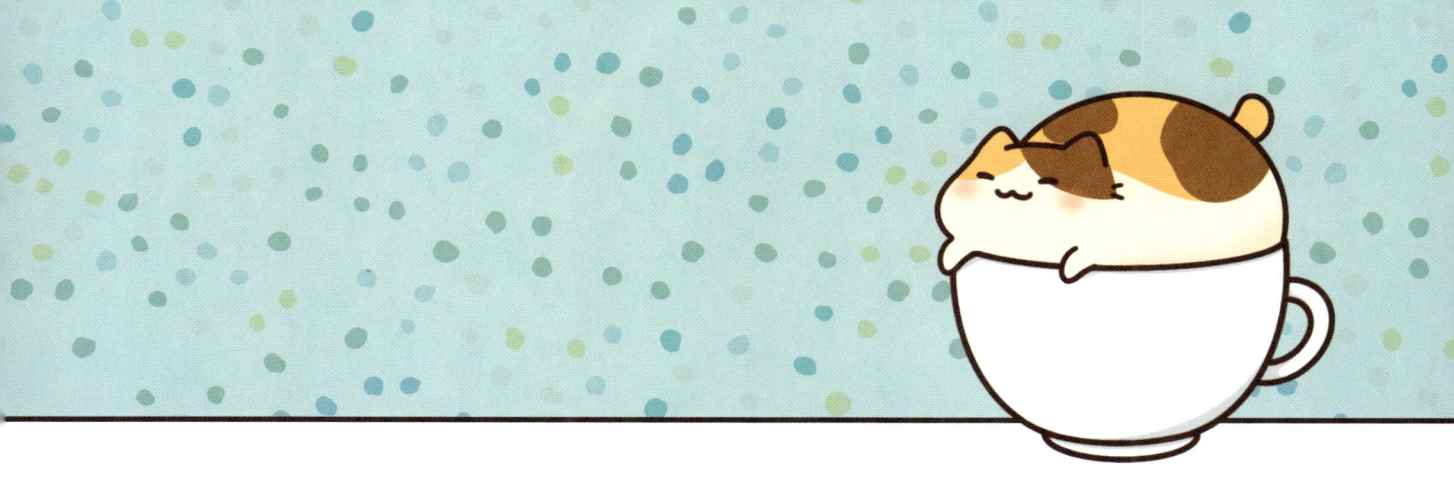

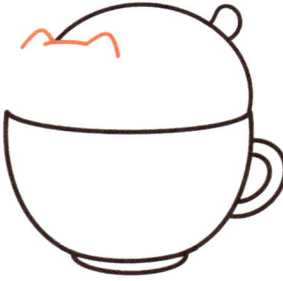

7. Draw the top of the head and the ears.

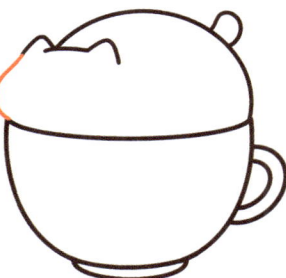

8. Draw the left side of the head.

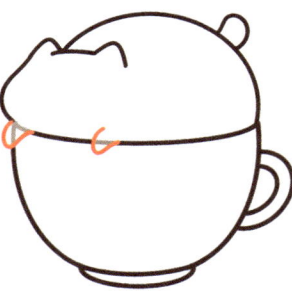

9. Add the front legs so they're hanging over the edge of the mug.

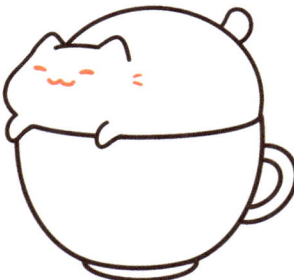

10. Finish by giving your cappuccino a fun facial expression.

KITTY CONE

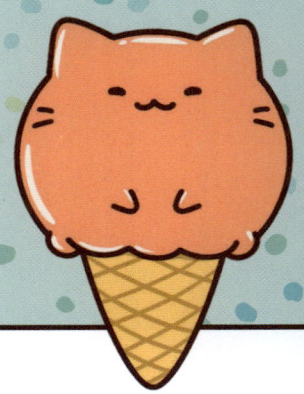

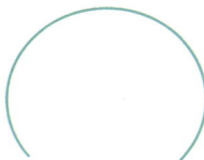

1. Draw an incomplete circle for the outline of the scoop of ice cream.

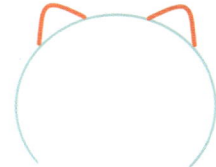

2. Add the ears.

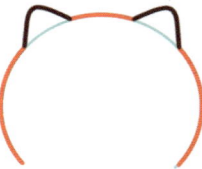

3. Draw the top and sides of the scoop of ice cream.

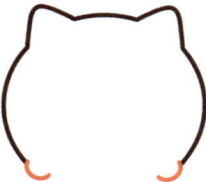

4. Add small curved lines to the bottom and sides of the scoop for the back legs.

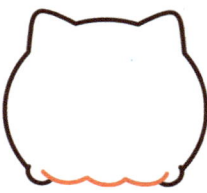

5. Connect the legs with a scalloped line for the scoop's bottom edge.

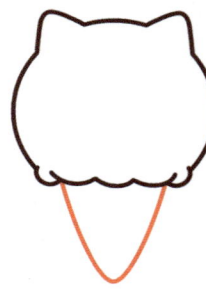

6. Draw a V shape for the cone.

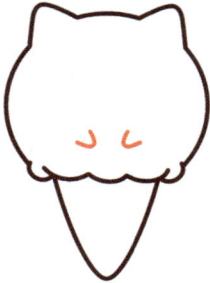

7. Add the front legs, facing each other, to the scoop of ice cream.

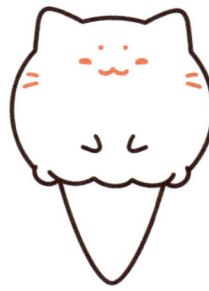

8. Finish by giving your ice cream cone a fun facial expression.

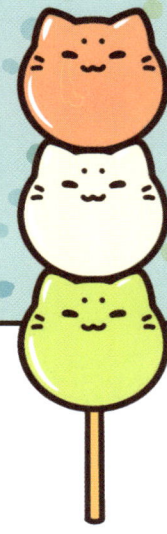

1. Draw three circles as outlines for the dango on top of one another.

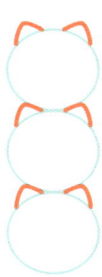

2. Add the three pairs of ears.

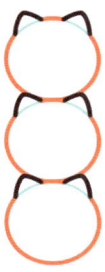

3. Draw the heads of the kitties.

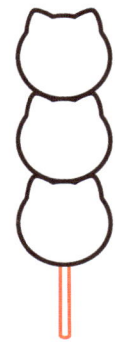

4. Add the stick below.

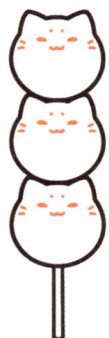

5. Finish by giving your dango three fun facial expressions.

KITTY ROLL

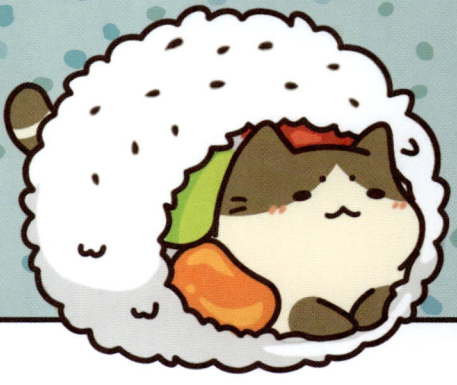

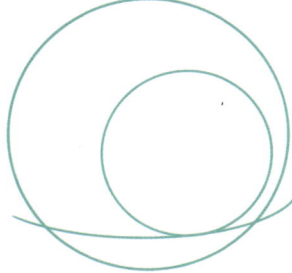

1. Draw the outline of the sushi roll with a smaller circle inside a larger circle. Add a slightly curved line across the bottom of the smaller circle.

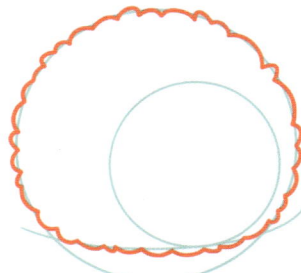

2. Draw the outside of the rice shape with jagged edges.

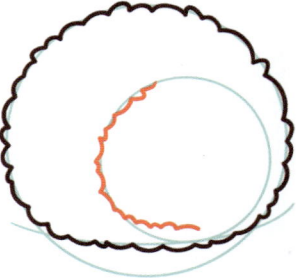

3. Draw the inner-left side of the rice shape with jagged edges.

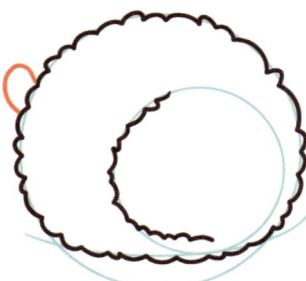

4. Add the kitty's tail.

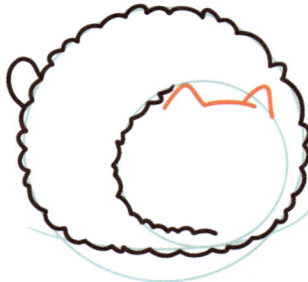

5. Draw the top of the head and the ears of the kitty.

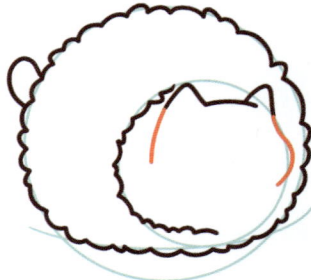

6. Draw the sides of the head.

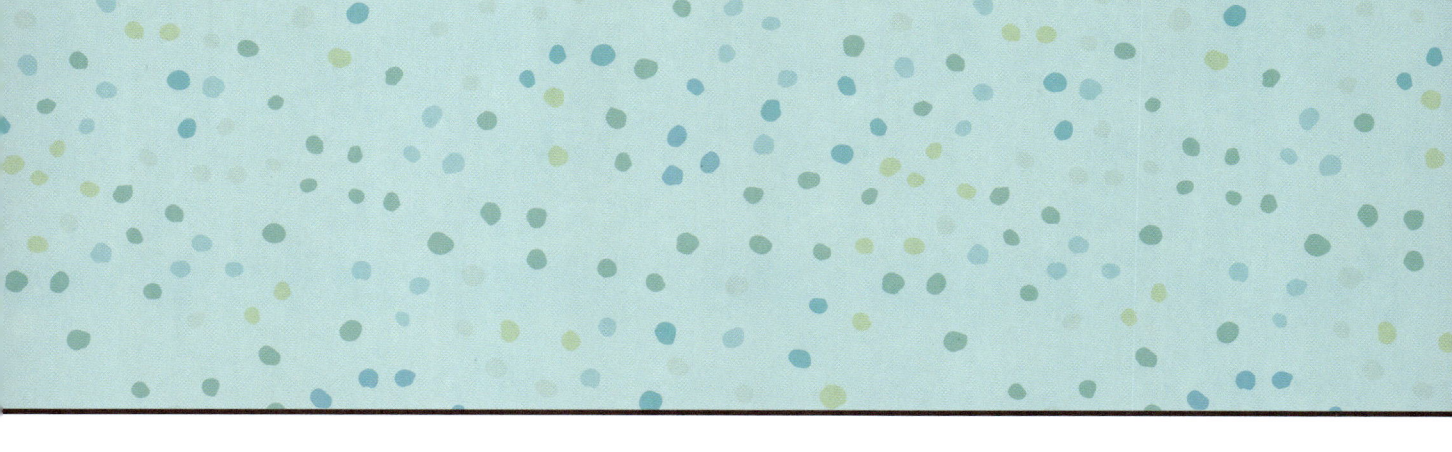

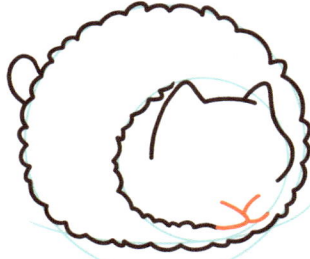

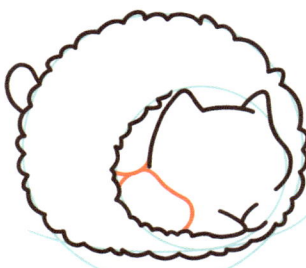

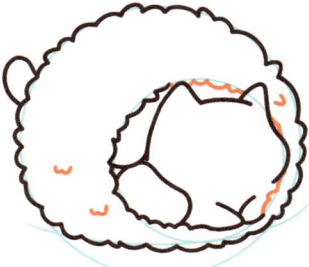

7. Add the front legs, touching each other.

8. Draw the vegetable shapes to the left of the kitty.

9. Draw the inner-right side of the rice shape with jagged edges. Add short curved lines to the outside of the rice for texture.

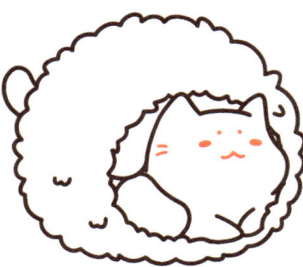

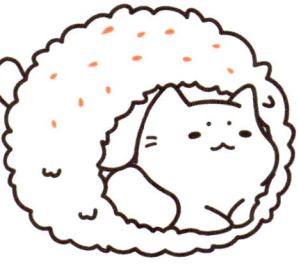

10. Give your sushi roll a fun facial expression.

11. Finish by drawing dashes on the top of your sushi roll for sesame seeds.

CUPCAT

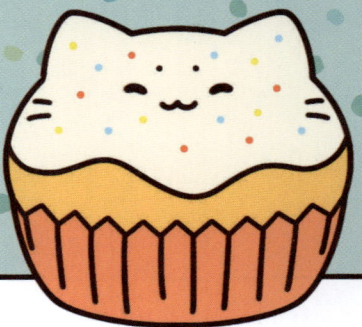

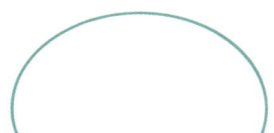

1. Draw a semioval for the outline of the cupcake top.

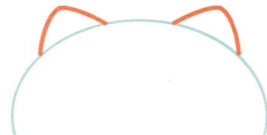

2. Add the ears.

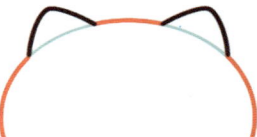

3. Draw the top and sides of the cupcake.

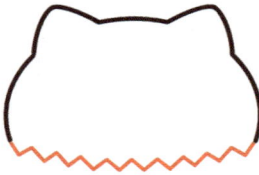

4. Connect the sides with a jagged line for the top of the cupcake liner.

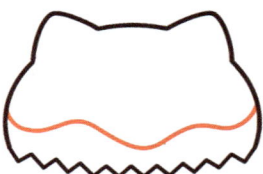

5. Draw a wavy line above that for the edge of the frosting.

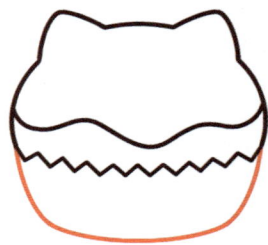

6. Draw the cupcake base.

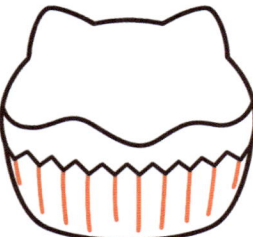

7. Add vertical lines to define the cupcake liner's folds.

8. Finish by giving your cupcake a fun facial expression.

Don't cry because it's over.
Smile because it happened.

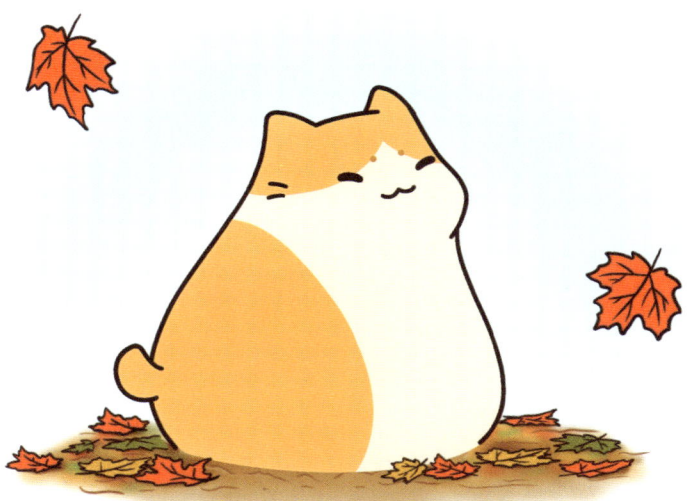

KITTY COLORING PAGES

Wait, there's more! Have fun coloring, adding markings, decorating, or even accessorizing the kitties on these pages. You can follow the color palette and markings on page 15 or be original. It's up to you!

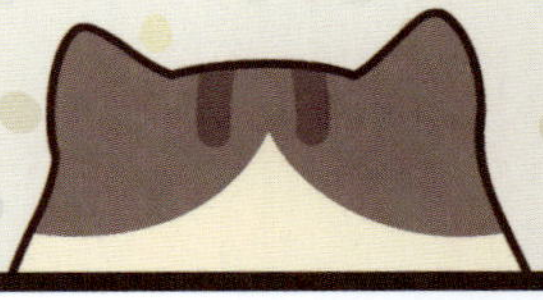

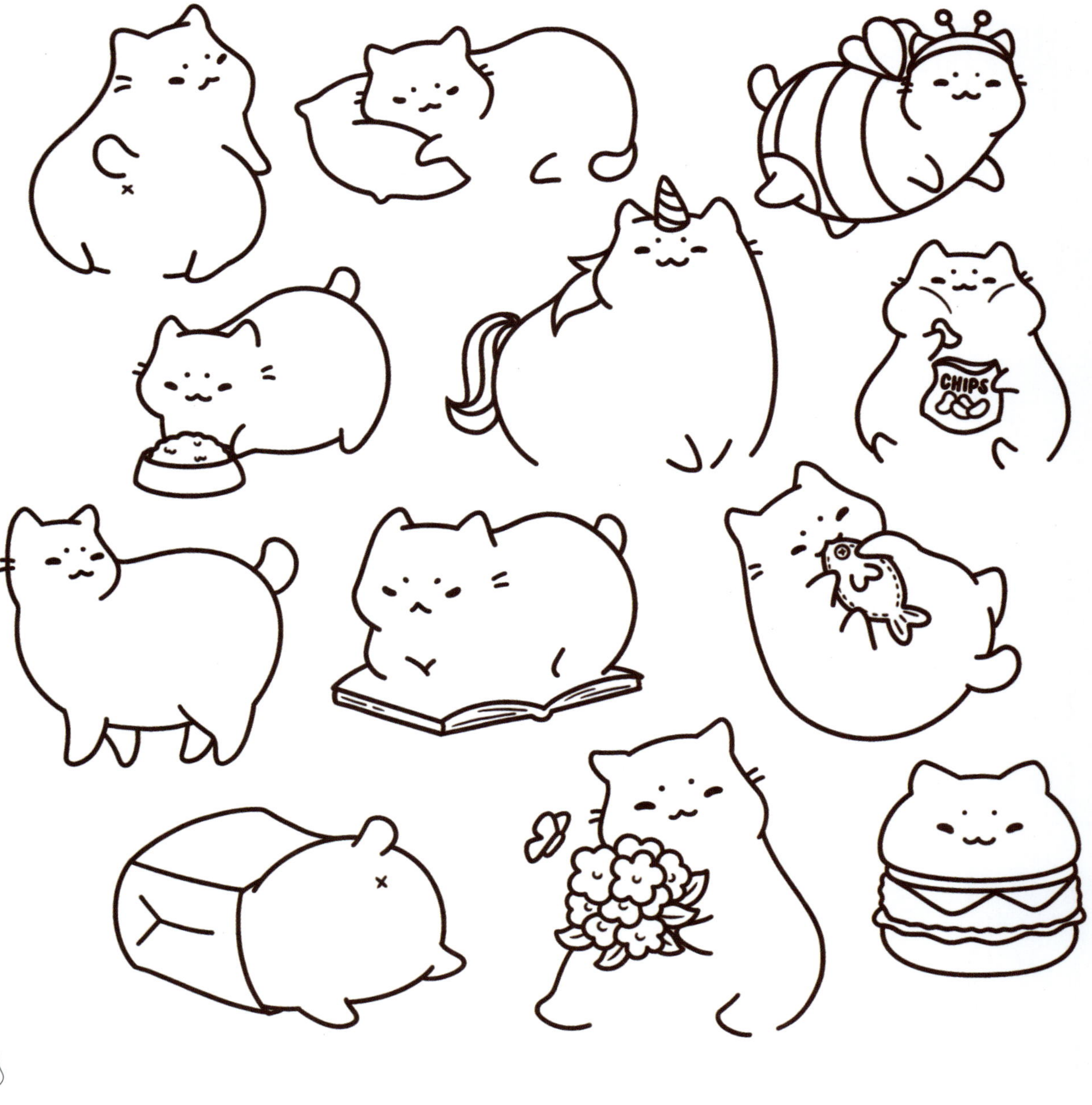

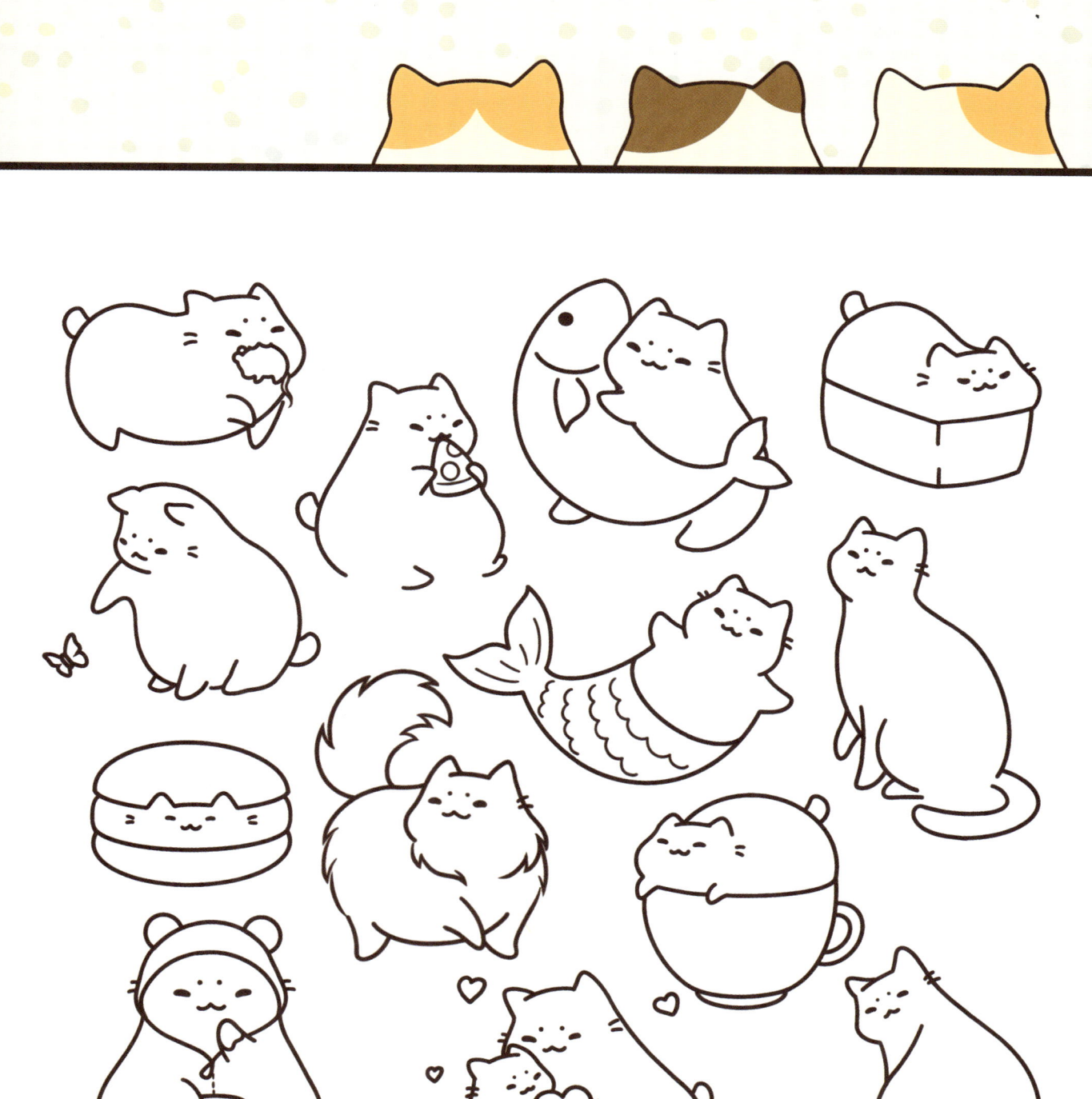

IF YOU ENJOYED KAWAII KITTIES, CHECK OUT THESE OTHER LEARN-TO-DRAW BOOKS!

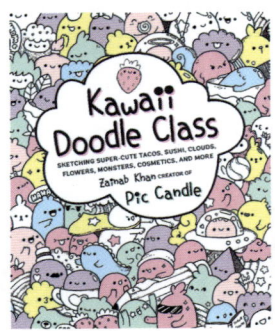

Kawaii Doodle Class
Sketching Super-Cute Tacos, Sushi, Clouds, Flowers, Monsters, Cosmetics, and More
ISBN: 978-1-63106-375-6

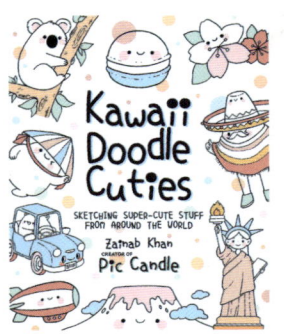

Kawaii Doodle Cuties
Sketching Super-Cute Stuff from Around the World
ISBN: 978-1-63106-568-2

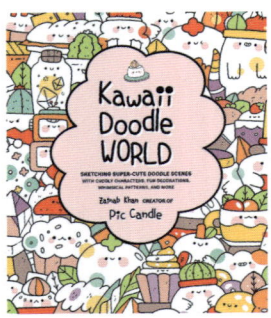

Kawaii Doodle World
Sketching Super-Cute Doodle Scenes with Cuddly Characters, Fun Decorations, Whimsical Patterns, and More
ISBN: 978-1-63106-697-9

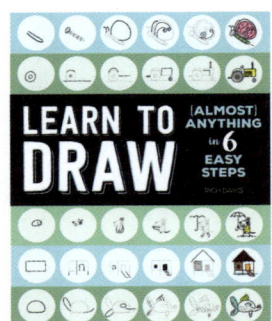

Learn to Draw (Almost) Anything in 6 Easy Steps
Sketching Super-Cute Stuff from Around the World
ISBN: 978-1-63106-716-7

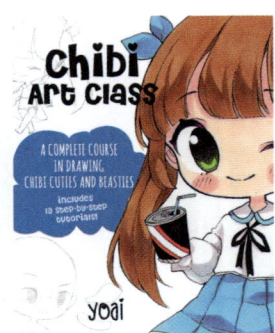

Chibi Art Class
A Complete Course in Drawing Chibi Cuties and Beasties
ISBN: 978-1-63106-583-5

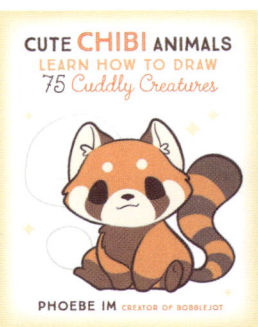

Cute Chibi Animals
Learn How to Draw 75 Cuddly Creatures
ISBN: 978-1-63106-729-7